What people are s
Clapperton and Phi

'*A dynamic and highly engaging presenter, Guy gives a unique perspective on collaborative working, providing a broad overview of a complex proposition – delivered in an easily digestible way. His refreshing approach to Unified Communications & Collaboration comes with plenty of humour.*'

— Doron Youngerwood,
Marketing Manager – Collaboration, Dimension Data

'*Guy is one of the most knowledgeable and engaging speakers when it comes to unified comms and collaboration. He spoke at our last event and was the ideal person to set the scene and get our collaboration event off to a good start.*'

— Annekathrin Hase, Director,
Strategy and Marketing – Mindlink Software

'*Philip was awarded the CCA Lifetime Achievement Award in recognition of the important contribution he has made to developing a strategic vision of the contact centre and knowledge worker of the future.*'

— Anne Marie Forsyth, Chief Executive, CCA

'*Philip Vanhoutte is a prime mover in improving workers' conditions to improve the business. The underlying principles of his work philosophy are giving freedom to employees to work where and when they want provided they produce results, they do not generate costs and that they are environmentally friendly*'.

— César Concepción Salza, editor, zonamovilidad.com (Spain)

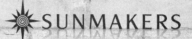
SUNMAKERS

Guy Clapperton
and **Philip Vanhoutte**

THE
SMARTER
WORKING
MANIFESTO

When, Where and How do you work best?

Text ©2014 Guy Clapperton and Philip Vanhoutte

THE **SMARTER WORKING** MANIFESTO
When, Where and How do you work best?

Published by Sunmakers, a division of Eldamar Ltd,
157 Oxford Road, Cowley, Oxford, OX4 2ES, UK
www.sunmakers.co.uk
Tel +44(0)1865 779944

Version 1.0

Designed by Ayd Instone
Cartoons by Simon Ellinas, cartoonsimon.com
Edited by Louise Bolotin
Authors photos by SaturEyes

ISBN: 978-1-908693-17-4

www.smarterworkingmanifesto.com

To all in the Smarter Working movement
– and all who want to join us!

Acknowledgments

It would be good to say that this book happened all by itself – that authors Guy and Philip got together, pooled their resources and it all came from our heads and nowhere else. This would of course be a load of phooey.

From my side the idea for this book came from a visit to Plantronics as editor of Unified Communications Insight (UCInsight.com), the fortnightly e-newsletter that supports the Connected Business Show (formerly UC Expo) run by Imago in London. I'm grateful to Mike England, my main contact at Imago Tech Media who organised the trip (and who's a thoroughly decent type to work with), and also to its owners Hugh Keeble and Mark Steele who I've known for (COUGH) years. At Plantronics I was impressed by the set-up which was radically different from anything I'd seen before. Managing Director Paul Clark kindly said he'd help if I were successful in finding a publisher for a book on the subject of smarter working – which, as a freelance, I'd been doing for years anyway.

That's where the initial impetus arrived from this end, although I'd been writing about employment and workplace as well as work technologies for years already. I'm grateful to Vic Keegan and Neil McIntosh as well as Jack Schofield, all formerly of the Guardian newspaper, for giving me the space to build up a decade or more of work on the topic, and more recently Alison Margiotta of the same publication for continuing to ask me to write on it right up to the present day. It wasn't just the Guardian – Richard Tyler at the Telegraph and a number of other commissioning editors at the Times, Independent and numerous other publications have kept me running and up to date on this fast-moving topic.

I was putting my proposal for a book together when I had one of those calls out of the blue from a long-established colleague, Paris Welton of Connected PR. Plantronics was her client, although she was unaware of my earlier visit to the Royal Wootton Bassett office. Based on work I'd done alongside her previously and my knowledge of the business, she was approaching me to co-write the very book I'd been considering, with Plantronics vice president Philip Vanhoutte (who, not being based in the UK, was equally unaware I already had such a project in my sights). They made it very clear indeed that this wasn't to be a Plantronics book but an independent one – and that's what we embarked upon.

Less than a year later I'm now looking at a completed manuscript and am pretty damned excited about it. I'm grateful to Paris for reintroducing me to Philip and letting me into a book which is so much better than I'd have put together by myself, and above all for project managing us as writers – if you're co-writing a book always, always have someone whose job it is to kick you up the backside once in a while! Louise Bolotin has been a tremendous copy editor and Ayd Instone is a great book designer. Tiffany Kemp (Devant.co.uk) was brilliant when it came to drafting and examining our authors' agreement and contract.

I'd also like to thank everyone who allowed me some of their time for interviews and looked over their quotes later. From Plantronics there were Tony Williams, Norma Pearce and George Coffin; from outside the company there were Andy Lake, Mark Mobach, Colin Rawlings, Annie Leeson, Luis Suarez, Dave Coplin, Julian Treasure, Richard Leyland, Louis Lhoest, Lynda Shaw and Tim Oldman. There were a couple whose diaries never quite matched up with ours – maybe for a second edition? And of course I must thank my wife Carol and daughter Charlotte for their continuing patience and for not laughing out loud when I said I was co-writing a book that mentioned work/life balance in any depth.

But mostly I have to thank Philip Vanhoutte, who agreed to work with me, stuck with me and most importantly who's actually implemented the principles and practices we discuss in this book in real life. For this reason, coupled with his encyclopaedic knowledge of the field, his contacts and willingness to throw his considerable industry clout behind it, it's 100 times the book I'd envisaged during that office visit, which seems so long ago. Thank you all – I hope the result is useful.

— Guy Clapperton

You are about to read the results of a journey that took lots of thoughts, research, belief and a bunch of enthusiasm and turned all of this into the printed (or on screen) word. Of course, this journey was not taken alone and I would like to thank some of my comrades who helped make this happen.

Firstly, my co-author, Guy Clapperton - it was a joy to work with such a seasoned wordsmith who shares a vision of smarter working. Also thanks to Philip Ross and Jeremy Myerson and their WorkTECH conferences who inspired me in the multidisciplinary field of Smarter Working (I felt like a curious kid in a candy store!) Tim Oldman and Annie Leeson provided perspective and depth through their groundbreaking research that shaped the smarter working Plantronics story.

Paris Welton, Liz Barber and Lisa Woodruff kept me on time with their energetic project management and support. To the Plantronics Europe and Africa team, a living laboratory of Smarter Working, it is a pleasure to work with and lead such an enthusiastic team. Of course, my boss Ken Kannappan has given me relentless encouragement and freedom to search for more engaging collaborative work environments.

Lastly but by no means least - I would like to thank my family, my wife Rosemie allows me to get fully immersed in my smarter working passion. This book is dedicated to Jan, Piet and Cindy, may they reach full realisation of their ambitions while working smarter.

— Philip Vanhoutte

Contents

Introductions

'Where and when do I work best?'

This is the question I've been trying to answer for the last two decades.

Blessed with the latest in mobile technology, I have experienced how some moments and places were just perfect for a particular job while others frankly sucked. I have learned that quiet early Sunday mornings were great to get ahead of the pack and make the most of the upcoming week. I learned that the awesome sunrise over Santa Cruz bay, observed from the balcony of a beach hotel, spurred crazy creativity and energy that crafted the most inspiring presentations I ever gave. I learned that nothing beats the bonding and learning over a meal together, that many conference calls were a big waste of time and why, oh why, were we commuting?

Nobody is expected to answer the where-when question in the same way but for many employers the answer has to be simple: people will work best pretty much where they are told. In general, this is some sort of company premises. In the case of many who will be reading this book, realistically we're talking about an office. And that's out of date.

In 2006, I attended WorkTech in London, where I met furniture manufacturer Vitra VP Tim Oldman who was conducting a study, later published as Work Topology, about understanding where business was being done. I was asked to participate and was interviewed by Annie Leeson. Among the questions was: Given the choice of where and when you could work, where would it be?

The study findings were eye-opening; creativity doesn't happen in traditional offices, you must have regular relaxation breaks at work, young people need productive open plan offices to immerse themselves in a business. Every type of information work behaviour has its own ideal space and time, not just depending on the type of activity but also fitting your personality profile. So get out of the office for some work, yet hurry back for key team work. It was then that I understood why I liked to work quietly on a cosy sofa on a Sunday morning: just being in a comfortable space, getting a lot done, being relaxed, nobody bursting in with anything urgent. But I also soon realized the limitations of working virtually.

I wanted to learn more about workspace experiments and commissioned Annie to research and write a report on what the best companies in the UK were doing about flexible working.

She spoke to a number of blue-chips and concluded that technology was important by all means – so was space – but the real catalyst was management style and above all trust-based, results-oriented work. In other words, you have to trust your colleagues to behave like adults and measure them by their output.

A year later, Plantronics had an opportunity to consolidate several buildings on an UK industrial estate into one. I was keen to offer space to suit the needs of new mobile and flexible office working styles and asked the staff, in an in-depth Leesman workspace satisfaction survey, about their information work behaviours and what they liked and didn't like about all aspects of their working environment.

The study was sobering; more than a third of the associates were not proud of their office to the extent that they would never show it to family or friends, let alone customers. The German office had awful acoustics that held back the energy and efforts of the inside sales team. There were plenty of red and orange alerts on the charts. Areas for improvement jumped right out to the management team, who were able to generate a briefing document of needs for IT, HR and Facilities in a matter of days.

Just around that time, Jeremy Myerson of the Royal College of Arts published his highly actionable research, *New*

Demographics, New Workspaces, with recommendations for four main work zone types, each with its own acoustic profile: concentration, collaboration, communication and contemplation. It suddenly all fell into place; we had the technology, we knew what the portfolio of activities was and how to lay out the smarter office interior. I said: 'OK guys, now we have all the elements – but the big change is going to be in work philosophy, so I'm asking Human Resources to coach the project because it's really about what we offer our associates, customers, partners ... all of them humans.'

We decided to create an acoustic temple, implementing Myerson's guidance, exactly to the demands of our associates. The project was completed in record time and the results were stunning: the Leesman workspace satisfaction index shot up from 63 to 84 in the post-occupation survey. Discretionary engagement with associates was boosted to a benchmark high, absenteeism dropped like a stone and we won a British Institute of Facilities Management Award in 2012. It felt like we were walking on water.

From the outset we had defined 'smarter working' as letting people work where and when as they wished as long as it delivered the right results, saved costs and respected the planet. Space, technology and people management worked together intensely to make the business more effective.

Essentially, Plantronics and some of the companies that take inspiration from us – as at 2013 we receive several visits per week from larger organizations investigating how we have made this new ethos work – have abandoned the idea of 9 to 5 office working completely. Nobody, literally nobody, including me, has a closed, personal office space. We ask our staff to consciously decide what is the best place and time to work, to master workspace portfolio management, every day.

Inevitably, it involves more than just deciding to 'work smart' one day and getting on with it. Management styles have to change. The topology of most established offices is unhelpful. There is a methodology to phasing this sort of ethos into the workplace. There are big implications for every element of the workplace, from technical infrastructure through recruiting the right people to career development. The results will be well worth the efforts: at Plantronics we saw halving absenteeism, 30% reduction in office space, 20% increase in customer and associate satisfaction and a noticeable increase in productivity.

This book will help managers embark on that journey. It will also help workers trying to make sense of the same journey to work smarter, with specific techniques and technologies that will help. Enjoy the ride!

– Philip Vanhoutte

'OK, I admit it – I find some of this a little baffling.'

People talk about flexible working, they talk about centring yourself around a task rather than a workplace. You'll find all of these things referred to and explored within the pages of this book. Only I've been doing it for more than 20 years and have found it bewildering that not everybody is doing so.

In my first two jobs, I worked in an office. I started as an administrator of a local charity, based in someone's house. They had a big place and I worked on what became their dining table in the evening – no doubt my posture and so forth was terrible but there wasn't so much information about that around in 1986. Or if there was, my employer was wise enough not to show it to me.

I then moved into journalism and had a little desk to myself. It was open plan and I got on well with the people around me for the first few years. Staff changes and a move in premises meant I was no longer in the same place after year three; it was more difficult to attract the attention of the editor (although the staff hadn't increased in number). I didn't function as well and eventually opted to go freelance.

At this stage, my productivity skyrocketed. I was able to choose my own computer subject to budget, I had my own motivation rather than a new boss who thought everything should be done his way to keep me going and I was paid for what I wrote rather than for how long I sat in a chair.

The technology also changed. I started to use handheld organizer devices and a mobile phone. Eventually the one could talk to the other and I could pick up messages while I was out. The device was called a PalmPilot and it would hold a few Word documents as well as addresses, calendar and emails. I once scandalized a commissioning editor at a publisher by turning up to a meeting without sheaves of paper; I had it all on the PalmPilot. He couldn't make the adjustment and, to be fair to him, it was probably too early to start working like that – but in the back of my mind there was the question: why do I need a desk at home taking a room up when I can carry all this stuff around in my pocket?

The technology is more readily available now. Arrive at a meeting with a laptop or tablet computer and people will accept fully that you're in work mode. And yet we're still substantially stuck in the mode of having a fixed workplace.

There can be good reasons for this, though, and smarter working isn't about getting rid of the office. It's about getting rid of having only one option. Many people find it easier to work if there's a distinct base of operations; somewhere they can see their colleagues, a building that's definitely where they work and meet. I could work in flexible working spaces the whole time and sometimes I enjoy the buzz. However, a lot of the time, when getting my head down and writing, I prefer to be by myself with few distractions. It's all about fitting the task to the place and how I'm going to work best. Applying this principle to an organization of any size is going to require thought and planning and, having been writing about the area for some time, I was delighted when Philip approached me to co-write this book as a result.

I was once told that Jean Paul Sartre said that it was insulting to be paid for your time rather than your achievements. I've Googled and come to the conclusion that someone wanted to make the point and just attached the name to the quote to add some weight and he probably never said it, but he should have. It's a useful maxim to live by; if someone can perform twice as many tasks as someone else in a given time, to the right standard, why shouldn't they have more time off or get paid twice as much? Maybe the person who is underperforming needs a little extra support, or would be better off based elsewhere? It is perhaps a little patronzing to assume that the two people should perform equally and are being managed well simply because they are located in the same space at the same time.

I've lived that way for a while. As a jobbing freelance I've had no option but I wouldn't go back. In this book, Philip and I explore how that freelance freedom, the ethic of getting jobs done in the best way possible for the individual and the organization, can apply to the largest organizations and we offer help to the managers and employees alike. It's an exciting thing to do – and we'd welcome your feedback on how you get on.

Guy Clapperton

Chapter One:

Find Your Space

WHERE DO YOU REALLY WORK? REALLY?

In this chapter we will look at:

- Why you work where you work.
- How office structures arrived and where they are heading.
- Justifying changes and achieving associate buy-in.
- Establishing metrics to measure progress.

Manifesto

As you'll have gathered from the title, this book aims to be a manifesto. People have been working 'flexibly', 'from home' or however else people want to dress a change of location up for quite a while as we go to press. But are they actually doing it properly – is it delivering business benefit as well as a personal level of satisfaction? In many cases the answer is no, because although the geographical shift is happening, they're not working any smarter than they were before they put the change in.

That's why this book has its very particular title. We're not talking about just working a little bit differently because you're in a different place. We're not talking about just doing things a bit more quickly because technology allows you to send emails from the train, or work for a call centre but use your home as your workstation. We're not talking about working from home every Friday religiously because it's a workplace habit. Those are the easy wins, but they also have easy pitfalls; the colleague who finds the train jostles too much to send a good email, the partner who swivels his or her eyes because someone else is 'working from home', the colleague who assumes 'working from home' means 'watching daytime TV' and resents the home-worker as a result, the employee who finds himself or herself instructed that they should work from home on Fridays when there's a meeting they should be having with actual people.

In other words, it is perfectly possible to have all the right tools in front of you for smarter working but to be using them in anything but a smart way. Each chapter that follows will contain actionable guidelines and suggestions, some of them straightforward and easy, and a number more complex. They will enable you to make better use of the tools available and recommend ways to really make smarter working fly.

It won't be oversold either as a business panacea or as an easy way of transforming a workplace – we've seen too many people assume this is some sort of quick fix. Like anything that's going to deliver real business benefit, it's hard work and a substantial undertaking.

In this first chapter, we'll look at three elements of your workplace and how to make it function better. The first is the job itself. The second is the people with whom you work, whether as an employer or simply as a colleague. The third is vital if you're going to get any benefit at all – yourself. None of us are corporate robots, much as some of the people in bluechip-land might want to pretend they are. Only once all three of these factors have been addressed will a genuine smarter working policy become a smart way of working.

Making this work well is our manifesto. We wish you luck on the journey. Let's dive in.

Why do you do what you do? And why on earth would you do it there?

Let's be more specific. Consider your own job – you might be a manager, a director, a journalist, a researcher, a manufacturer, an actor, anything. But if you're reading this book then the chances are that you're in employment of some sort and you have a reason to do what you do. Very probably 'to make money' is among your objectives. Hopefully, you enjoy your job and find it fulfilling, too.

The more interesting question is why you do it where and how you do it. For some people this will be easy: 'I'm an actor and it kind of helps if I rehearse with the other actors, the director and then turn up at the theatre/on set when I'm needed' is pretty unarguable.

But what if you do information work? Why do you go to work every day and why travel somewhere at all? Is it necessarily the best place to perform the tasks your organization requires of you? Consider a moment. You're an accountant, we'll say.

You go into the office after a long commute and sit in front of a computer, number-crunching. You take calls from clients and maybe even do a bit of video conferencing to talk face to face.

In the 21st century, why was it necessary to do that commute?

Nobody is saying there can't be reasons. You might have a meeting you need to attend in person – one which frankly wouldn't work without your actual physical presence. You might have a client who insists on visits and who has no premises suitable to receive you. You might – and this is perfectly valid, no matter what the flexible working evangelists tell you – work better with the buzz of a few people around you. That's a perfectly valid reason for going into the office – because you like it there and that's where you work best.

For many people, though, it's not the right option at all. They have a home office, a study, they could use perfectly happily as long as the technology is in place. Their phone is either attached to their computer rather than a landline (or could be) or a mobile and they don't need, in any way, to be in the office to receive calls. The chatter of colleagues may be a distraction during head-down time.

Wouldn't it be better if their employer were to give them a set of objectives and desired results and leave them to sort out how it's going to work by themselves? As long as deadlines are met and the business is not affected adversely – and as we'll see, a positive impact is far more likely anyway – why are you forcing your people to come into a particular building, for which (let's remember) you're paying?

And look, how did we get here in the first place?

Planning to design your office for complete flexibility is great in theory but remarkably few people have the luxury of starting from scratch. The vast majority have an established workplace already and need to make adaptations to it so that it can be used in different ways.

In fact, let's consider that word. 'Workplace'. What does it actually mean? The answer for many people is straightforward enough; it's the place you go to work. This in turn has all sorts of cultural and technological assumptions behind it. The idea that there is one place for work is only one of them. This is based around the notion that working and private lives are entirely separate, which the authors believe is a fallacy in the modern world.

But we're getting ahead of ourselves. How did this 'office' thing start in the first place?

A history of the office

'Office' comes from the Italian Uffizi. Probably.

The first recognizable offices were in the industrial age. Possibly. The structure was a lot like a prison cell; the idea was that the worker would be absolutely supervised and contained. Office halls didn't literally have employees chained to their desks but one can only imagine it felt like it (not that we should be judging events that took place two hundred years ago through the eyes of the 21st century – that's a cultural mismatch waiting to happen).

Professor Mark Mobach, of Groningen University in the Netherlands, is an authority on the development of the modern workplace and he confirms there is an element of ambiguity about where this stuff actually started. 'We aren't really sure where or when the "cellular" idea started. Basically some people say it stems from the monks, others say it traces back to the Uffizi.' In the Uffizi – now of course a gallery in Florence – a duke in the Medici family had many landlords working for him and he wanted them to be close by. He created offices in Florence with a cellular structure, so from the word go (or avanti, we suppose) the office structure was all about power. 'He wanted to directly influence the people working for him who would have been responsible to him.'

This basic structure stuck for a very long time. Mobach: 'In the last century there were many developments that caused many aspects of current workplace design. We have to be aware of the basic idea of an office. A hundred years ago you would have seen mostly product-oriented organizations, manufacturers producing physical goods. So the people related to the administration would work in offices. For other organizations, like the Larkin Soap factories, the larger offices were like a factory in their own right with an open plan.' Offices at this point started to be designed around the workflow within a company; there would be a logical, sequential order to where people were placed. 'The office of Darwin Martin, one of the directors, was at the heart of this structure, exhibiting his influence and power to the working floor. At the time in many companies there would also be spaces where only the board of directors would have an office, decorated and with a cellular structure.'

A major shift then happened when the developed world started to move a great deal more towards the service industries as a mainstream business. It is in this sort of structure that the office becomes a status symbol; the top management has to have the best/top office, and if numerous American movies of the 1960s are to be believed, their own washroom. With a key. 'You can still see that. As the service industry grew it became normal that people worked in offices,' says Mobach.

Office models

Although this book will encourage you to focus on the task and the professional worker rather than the physical area in which they function, it is worth outlining some of the different models of workspace that exist a little more formally than we have done above. The standard work on this is *Space to Work: New Office Design* by Jeremy Myerson and Philip Ross. This is a superbly illustrated and well thought out guide as to the different sorts of work premises businesses have used. It includes:

Academies

Effectively working campuses, designed to eliminate much of the hierarchical nature of the old workplace and instead encourage a collegiate, collaborative ethos. The architects will typically have designed them to encourage movement rather than compartmentalize different departments and hierarchies.

Guilds

A 'professional cluster', say Myerson and Ross, allowing people to group themselves together within their individual disciplines according to the organization that employs them.

Once again the idea is to encourage and facilitate ideas being bounced around in a collaborative environment – the guild model lends itself to the shared working space as well as the single-company building.

Agora

From the name of the central point of the Ancient Greek city, these are open spaces and marketplaces that become the focal point in their own right. These are very often populated by large statement buildings, and might well include co-working spaces. We will see more of co-working later in the book.

Lodge

This is effectively a high-register name for a home office, home industry, or any combined living and working space. Myerson and Ross highlight working lofts in the US, UK, Japan and elsewhere. These buildings are distinctive for having been designed with both work and living in mind from the start rather than putting an office into an established living space.

Each of these types of building has something to offer to the right organization and there has been no consensus as to

TENSIONS AT WORK
SPACE STRATEGIES FOR KNOWLEDGE WORKERS

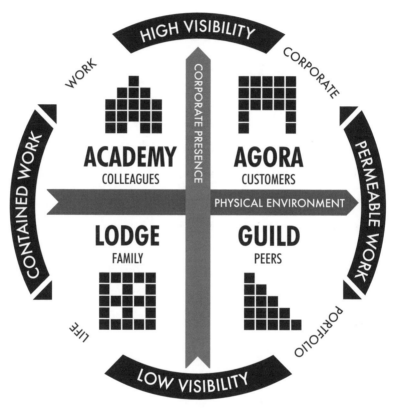

Source: *Space to Work, New office design*, Jeremy Myerson and Philip Ross

which sort of building fits which business. You are as likely to find a guild structure in a creative industry as in manufacturing; campuses might apply to a bank just as easily as they would a major software house, and any of them can decide they're big enough to deserve an agora or at least part of one. Equally, each can take advantage of a lodge for smaller, more departmental tasks. It is simply worth being aware of which sort of premises you have on your shortlist when considering where a business should be based.

Space specifically for your job

So if you're planning some work activity, why not start with that activity rather than automatically go to a physical location to perform it? Start with the job – we'll come onto a definition of 'activity-based working' later, but for the moment just assume you're neutral as to where you perform your tasks.

It's here that the notion of work topology becomes a very useful concept indeed. Originated by Annie Leeson, who we'll encounter in a later chapter as well, it involves taking each task and looking at where they are best performed. This includes a guide to the ideal spaces for each sort of work behavior or activity to take place, including:

- Birth of an idea – for which people ideally need to be alone and stimulated.

- Deliberation and contemplation – which develops the idea and needs an element of seclusion. Leeson suggests this is best done somewhere that is not the office; experiences of companies building specific contemplation areas into an office suggest a flexible approach may be better.

- Fission-fusion – the idea of bringing ideas together after they have been developed independently for a while is an important concept in flexible working. This needs to be done together somewhere.

- Immersion – steeping oneself in the company culture needs to happen in an open plan office.

- Reflexive thinking – this is best done in busy or public areas, the classic ideas coming together by the coffee machine scenario.

- Joining forces – ideally done on neutral territory, somewhere away from the main work zone.

- Refuelling – clearly this needs to be done away from the office.

PRODUCTIVE INFORMATION
WORK BEHAVIOURS

Source: *The Topology of Work,* Annie Leeson

It's quite notable that very few of these forms of activity, other than the obvious immersion into office culture, really have a 'you must do this task here' edict attached.

So, when you're managing your tasks for yourself or apportioning them to employees, do you consider whether you should be performing them somewhere specific? Or do you look to the employee and ask 'where and when would you be best able to perform this task'?

Your evolving workspace

A traditional office has four types of space:

- The private office: typically for managers

- The shared office for 2-6 people, mostly working for the same function and often working as a team as part of a workflow

- Landscape or open plan offices, with no walls, often with rows of people and in many cases with little or no attention to good acoustics

- Meeting rooms of various sizes

As you will have noticed over the past few years, the topology of work is changing with greater use of spaces outside the office, more flexible use of space within the office, reduction of underutilized office space, less ownership of fixed workstations and the advent of more collaborative, community spaces. This has an impact on the way we work as no desk-ownership and more desk-sharing is on the rise, providing more choice over where to work and more variety of work settings to choose from.

This can bring huge benefits in greater autonomy and personal growth, control over how and where you work best, more variety of workplace options, better tools for working outside the office and ultimately better productivity in the right spaces.

The key is using the right spaces for the right activities: to work as comfortably and productively as possible.

So, how would you characterise the work activity you do?

- Working alone versus working with others

- Process-driven versus creative thinking

- Specialist tools or materials needed versus only basic work tools needed

- Requires intense concentration versus external stimulus

- Can be done in small chunks or needs one long session

And what about your personal working style: how do you like to work, and how do you feel about it? Do you:

- Want a 'buzzing' atmosphere or prefer complete peace and quiet?

- Possibly need some support or prefer to do certain work yourself?

- Find the work really engaging or do you need discipline to do this work?

- Prefer to be around people or rather like to be on your own?

- Need to look outside for ideas or need to think deeply to get ideas?

Information processing

One of the major parts of the original medieval Italian offices that dictated their structure was the information technology available at the time. By modern standards it was virtually non-existent: pens of some form, paper, desks, travel by horse. It's a wonder nobody thought of Googling to see if there was anything better.

Essentially, the absence of a means of collaborating by any means other than presenteeism meant that it was the only option. If all of the ledgers and figures were on paper and held in one area, locked away overnight, then there is no question; the people putting them together had to be in that building with them.

The baffling thing about that technical element of the early office is that it's completely gone away. No, wait; that's not baffling, that's just progress. The baffling thing is that in so many cases the removal of so many technical barriers has made so little difference to working practices (deadlines have moved from 'ouch' to 'you must be joking', we admit that) that they may as well not have happened.

Look at examples in which people absolutely have to come to the office. There are many. In fact, in 2013 internet company Yahoo! decided that everybody should come in because the buzz was better to work with than trying to do it alone (we'll come to why you don't need to feel alone in a second). So, let's say someone comes into their workplace in the modern world. There's a good chance they'll check their emails before they arrive because this is easy to do with a BlackBerry, iPhone, Android phone, Windows phone, tablet – people have emailers coming out of their ears these days. Many people carry two: one for personal use and one for work.

So if you've already started working and are mentally in the office why is a commute necessary?

Nonetheless, they come into the office because that's what the bosses say they must do and they have to earn a living. Rather than get a pen or quill and paper out for a physical ledger, they log on to a spreadsheet – it's much the same thing. They collaborate electronically because they're all looking at the same view of the same document.

Now pause a second. They are logged in and looking at a view of a spreadsheet. There is no reason, repeat literally no reason, they should be looking at this through any particular screen as long as it works on another. The chances are it's browser-based so could be seen on a smartphone. This could be too small but is it too small for a tablet? For a designer, perhaps it is. But is there a reason they shouldn't view this in a remote office, or even using their home internet connection?

Activity-based working

So maybe we should scrap this 'desk' idea all together. Or if we don't scrap it completely, how about getting rid of the fixed office desk as a useful notion?

Philip Ross, whom we've already mentioned as co-author of *Space to Work* with Jeremy Myerson, advocates 'activity-based working'. In this scheme, literally nobody has a fixed desk in an organization. In a paper entitled "Death of the Desk", he outlines his belief that people will simply move from desk to desk using their mobile technology within a business, working not where they have a fixed place but where the task at hand takes them. Arguably, this is very similar to the old professional idea of 'hot-desking', which consisted of moving around buildings in much the same way immediately the technology was available to allow people to do so. It is possible that this came to very little in the very early part of this century because it was too early; the technology was certainly available but the company cultures were a good deal less clear.

So, for this chapter we'll stick with looking at the fixed office rather than the remote or mobile worker – there will be more on them in Chapters Two and Three. We'll assume everybody needs a headquarters or a branch office of some description. And we'll first examine the question: how easy is it to work in your building? Many businesses start off with the idea of desk space and fixed phones and overlook other important elements.

The people you work with

The second element of ascertaining whether a workplace is right for someone is the people you deal with. We can extend this to mean the company culture overall, as this will be dictated to a large extent by the folks in it. But let's not overlook prestige.

It's still the case today that the biggest businesses like to have the grandest premises, albeit not to the same extent as in the 1980s. Travel down the M4 corridor in England, get off at the right exit and you'll find Microsoft's buildings. Sorry, did we say buildings? It's a campus and described as such.

Now, we're not anti-Microsoft by any means. It's a huge concern that needs a series of buildings if it's going to work at all in the way it has grown up doing. Let's take another example from the technology field, Google. Until 2014 situated in the UK at the heart of London's Victoria (and elsewhere, it has more offices), these are premises that say 'we can afford this'.

Google is a fun example because it has put a little quirkiness into its office. Not, perhaps, to the extent that an example from a colleague had; a marketing company had bought a car to park in reception. No, you didn't read that wrongly. Someone had considered that good use of a five-figure sum was buying a car to stick in reception and leave it there permanently – nobody ever moved this car. Which is fine, as long as the company is doing well; very few people would welcome the sight of that sort of extravagance parked in reception as they made their way out following the decision to let a few people go because of cash flow. (We stress again in case any lawyers are reading, this one wasn't Google!)

Equally, there are instances in which 'pared back' is effectively a statement about who works in a place and what it's like. Matthew's Yard in Croydon, south of London, is a shared working space, converted from a warehouse, dedicated to technology start-ups. The atmosphere is positively anti-corporate, there are a number of benches rather than desks in some areas and the local internet radio station is squirreled away in a corner behind glass doors. There is a good coffee bar but it's very much 'rough and ready' for beginners rather than the sparkly, gleaming office spire. This is as much a statement about who works there as anywhere else. Sticking with a UK example, co-working space Level 39 in London's Canary Wharf is a slick space in the City; even the coffee machines are operated by an iPad. Both make statements about the sort of worker who will be there and the stage they'll be at.

'Office as a statement' is very much still with us. Quirky, pared back or as prestigious as the Trump Tower, many people will use their premises as a means of displaying their capability and good taste (they believe) to the maximum size of audience.

The purpose of a workplace is arguably to invite the employees to work in it. So it needs to be the right workplace for the right people.

Q and A: **Steelcase**

American furniture maker Steelcase has it all – a quirky workplace and a product that makes workplaces themselves more comfortable. We asked a spokeswoman how the company had achieved its aims so far.

Q: Steelcase makes furniture. How has the increased awareness of the need for smarter working changed demand and designs?

A: Work today has fundamentally changed. The world is more global, mobile and 24/7. As organizations and individuals are learning how to navigate the waters of this global, complex and interconnected business environment, smart leaders understand the power of real estate to help organizations create, innovate and drive growth.

This insight has been pivotal in Steelcase's ability to face today's business challenges: complexity, global competition for customers and talent, cost pressures and the driving need to innovate. With pressures like these, the workplace is an opportunity waiting to be discovered by most businesses today.

Innovation requires a more agile organization and a more collaborative workforce, and a workplace that encourages both. When designed and equipped to meet the challenges of the new, interconnected world, the workplace can help shape the kinds of employees that leaders want most: creative and highly engaged workers, who can collaborate with teammates anywhere in the world, iterate work easily and make quicker decisions. Steelcase helps its clients understand how the workplace can augment human interactions to foster more creative, and innovative employees.

Q: Your corporate video suggests your identity is shot throughout your premises. How do you make this happen?

A: Leading organizations care about their purpose and they know how to make their brand visible through the spaces where they bring their people together. They create destinations designed to augment human interactions, places where people can come together to do their best work whether alone or individual.

As organizations fight to thrive in this global, complex and interconnected world, many are finding that the workplace is an underutilized asset. An intentionally designed workplace is a powerful tool for driving global integration, building culture and augmenting the human interactions for creative and innovative employees.

To do this organizations must create places that inspire their people to bring the purpose to life. That means leading organizations must understand people need technology, people need people and people need space that brings technology and people together. They do this by offering choice and control over how and where people work through creating a palette of place (a range of settings organized into intentional zones), a palette of posture (a range of solutions that encourage people to sit, stand and walk) and a palette of presence (a variety of ways to connect to colleagues around the world).

Q: Many companies have specific areas for specific types of task – contemplation, concentration, communication, collaboration, can all be done best in different places. How do you make this work in your own business – or do you have a different approach?

A: Exactly. Business today is more challenging, tasks more varied. People move constantly from focused individual work to one-on-one meetings, project sessions to impromptu collaborations, a series of planned and unplanned interactions throughout the day, and 5 o'clock is no longer day's end for most workers with colleagues spread across time zones and countries. A recent IBM study of human resource executives found that 80 per cent of organizations want workers to collaborate more. Given the increasingly distributed and mobile workforce, however, they aren't quite sure how to do it: 78 per cent of executives want their organizations to be better at it.

At Steelcase we believe in giving workers choice and control over where and how employees work. This recognizes that people need individual 'I' spaces and group 'we' spaces. It also breaks the paradigm that all individual spaces should be assigned or owned and that all group work spaces should be shared. The range of spaces in an interconnected workplace need to support focused work, collaborative work, socializing and learning.

Q: How do you go about getting employee buy-in when, say, you want to change the work space around a task – or indeed if you want them all to adopt standing or even walking desks as a policy affecting employees?

A: Good point, and that could be a concern, our advice would be though to first offer choice and control. Workers need choice and control over where and how they work – we would advise not to force anyone to do anything. There are times when you need a quiet space for contemplative work, time when you need collaborative work and others when you want some social interactions. Some workers want to stand while others want to sit, some need to be more mobile, while some work best in an 'owned' workstation. Steelcase believes workers need choice and control which includes a palette of place, palette of posture and palette of presence throughout the day.

Q: *If you could change three things about the way companies in the US go about planning their working space, what would they be?*

A: 1. Offer choice and control over where and how they work. Organizations need to provide a variety of spaces for the variety of tasks throughout the day. Technology enables people to work anywhere today, so the workplace has to do more and be more. It has to bring people together in an intentional way and be designed to meet their needs.

2. Provide a variety of I and We spaces. In today's open plan world, the pendulum has swung too far, privacy and

53

individual work is just as important as group. Organizations need to also think about the diversity of thought within an organization – open plan collaborative spaces don't work for everyone, all the time. Remember to include private spaces for quiet, focused, individual work.

3. Consider the wellbeing of your people. There is a global assault on worker wellbeing today and Steelcase research revealed a new definition of how organizations must solve this problem – they must think about the physical, physiological and cognitive wellbeing of their people. This means thinking about things like authenticity, belonging, optimism, mindfulness, vitality and meaning of employees.

Q: In terms of workplaces in the US, what's changed recently, what needs to change?

A: In the past, people had to go to the office to go to work. If they weren't in the building they couldn't connect with co-workers, the company's IT system or printed files; if they weren't in the building, they weren't working. Then technology cut the tethers to specific locations for work, the global economy became everyone's marketplace and cutting expenses became paramount.

Technology tantalized us with the idea that we could save money by rethinking our approach to work and traditional concepts about the workplace. Did we need buildings at all? Could workers simply work from home and communicate virtually? Could the company substantially reduce its real estate and its inherent costs by implementing alternative workplace strategies?

But many companies quickly found out the answer was no. People need people, people need technology and people need spaces that bring people and technology together.

Today some companies have started mandating that people come back to the office as a way to drive collaboration and rebuild a sense of connectedness to the organization.

Despite plenty of pros and cons cited for co-location versus distributed work, real estate professionals agree that the discussion has elevated the awareness of how much the physical environment drives organizational performance and business results.

Leading organizations know this means more than just bringing people together in buildings that bear their name. It means going beyond the aesthetics of the environment to creating places that actually help people engage more fully in their work, help build trust with distributed co-workers and allow people to innovate faster. Companies have learned and now they're asking how to create work environments where people really want to come to work.

The challenge today is creating spaces where people want to come to work, to connect with each other and that augment their interactions to provide more creative, innovative and collaborative organizations.

You and your space

The other element you need to understand is simple – you, or the individual to whom you're assigning the work. Assuming you have the right person for the job – and if you don't, that falls outside this book's remit – how do you place them correctly?

In the book, *Work, Happiness and Unhappiness*, author Peter Warr highlights several different personality types. An emeritus professor of psychology, Warr understands just how differently people will react given different stimuli. The differences to which he points are cultural, demographic and occupational on the one hand; one person might value more personal involvement in the running of a company whereas another might not, for example. He examines personality, genes and happiness – some people really do seem genetically predisposed to be happier than others, some will thrive in a crowded environment and some will not.

Crucially he identifies the difference between introverts and extroverts – and their different needs. The extrovert may want more social contact and will enjoy bouncing ideas around different people, so their idea of an ideal place to do work – subject to being in the right place for the task – will be different from that of the introvert (of course the introvert may be more inclined to opt for a more 'private' role in the first place).

Hear the difference

Meanwhile, once someone is in the right place, doing the right job, they will start to notice things going right and some going wrong. And one of the major factors affecting whether the workplace is functioning well or not is the noise level. There needs to be a sensitivity to space acoustics and indeed some acoustic zoning.

Office acoustics are more important than a lot of people understand. Take a typical casual meeting encounter. You grab a coffee and sit in an open plan café, discussing this and that – and struggling at times to make yourselves heard. This is not because of any massive background noise – there aren't many people around. It is because of the passing noise. The architects will have made two classic errors:

Wooden floors. Although the coffee area is carpeted, the walk floors are made of wood and as such anyone wearing clicky heels makes quite a noise. This is exacerbated by the second problem.

Glass panels instead of low walls under staircase handrails, overlooking a floor below. It looks very dramatic and glass walls are often in place in modern buildings. People like them, they look swish – and they reflect any noise straight back, echoing around like anything.

Without being ageist in any way (at all), the younger of the two co-authors of this book was in his late forties for the above casual sit-down and we can both vouch that in the natural order of things, hearing deteriorates as you age. This means the more background noise there is – perhaps noise that would not bother a 21-year-old – the more your senior colleagues are going to start to struggle. Buildings from materials that encourage noise is going to make life trickier than it needs to be. This can be overcome with planning.

It's worth skipping forward a little and reflecting on what Julian Treasure, sound and communications guru and author of the book *Sound Business*, says about buildings in which work takes place and their architecture. We'll meet him in a little more depth later in the book, but during our interview he reflected that, 'when you commission an architect to design a building, the first thing they do is to produce a lot of drawings. They never tell you what it will sound like.' To be fair to architects, probably very few people ask them about the sound and acoustics, but what's the biggest distraction when you're trying to work?

Case Study: **Plantronics**

George Coffin, facilities manager at Plantronics, explained the process of designing the office from the ground up. Acoustics were in the plan from the first day, as was the idea of absentee non-office workers. He explains that putting together a building for a flexible workforce consisted in Plantronics' case of first auditing the work actually being done and finding out who'd be working on site at a given time. This was as important as finding out what they would need to store. 'Everybody who would be working on site for three days a week or more was provided an open plan desk,' he says. Storage space costs were at a premium; it was possible to cut the requirements down by educating people not to store personal effects at work, which people often do, and to pare back the amount of things people needed in the first place. This, once again, was a matter of audit.

Central to the task – and something that can be duplicated by any number of enterprises – was putting together the acoustic offering. This was made complex by some of the initial requirements. As Plantronics was commissioning a new building it wanted to put a few revolutionary ideas in place. Coffin confirms that the company did not want too many walls or corridors and it had an idea to get rid of as many doors as possible. 'Doors, corridors and walls all take up space and therefore waste money,' he says. 'Every piece of space costs money and it's my job as a facilities person to save the business costs.'

The real meat of the project came in when the acoustics had to be built in, though. He employed Colin Rawlings, technical director of specialist company Acoustix, who explains there are a number of typical mistakes architects will have made. '"Plantronics' requirements were fairly normal but usually I have to put the improvements in after the building is finished,' he says. 'It was unusual to be putting it in at the design stage.' It's not unusual for him to arrive at a premises and find it full of glass and hard surfaces such as wood, which will bounce and amplify a great deal of noise around the enterprise.

There are a number of specifics his company was able to fit which can just as easily be put in to an existing building as a new project.

- Ceiling tiles: Noise bounces off many surfaces and the ceiling is often one of them. By specifying an acoustic absorbing ceiling tile Acoustix was able to neutralize at least one surface as a source of noise.

- Cellular space: The objective here is speech clarity and speech privacy. Teleconferencing in particular is not helped by sound reflecting in a meeting room because it causes echoes and reduced intelligibility.

  Using acoustic foam on the walls behind visually attractive printed graphics reduces the echo or reverberation. BASF makes the foam Plantronics uses.

  Check that all walls are sealed to the ceiling and that doors have a good seal on them. Sound literally leaks and, like water, if there is a space in which it can get through, it will. 'A lot of people spend a lot of money on partitions but they're often wasting it because they don't have the right door seals,' says Rawlings.

- Open plan: Concentrating while sitting in an open plan office is difficult if there is a lot of noise.

  Putting absorption into the ceiling is a good first start.

  Using carpet rather than hard wood floors.

Put absorption onto the walls in a closed meeting room with an acoustic foam covering (this can itself be covered with graphics so that it doesn't look too industrial if desired).

Blocking material can be put up as screens on desks.

Background sound: cover with a sound masking system to mask unwanted noise.

In essence: remember the Acoustics ABC:

A – Absorb noise close to the source either with sound absorbing panels such as the BASF foam or using a good sound absorbing ceiling tile.

B – Block the direct path of sound, door seals etc in meeting rooms and desk screens in the open plan.

C – Cover, mask unwanted and distracting noise by raising the background sound level using a sound masking system.

Plantronics implemented the highly actionable research from Jeremy Myerson's *New Demographics, New Workspaces* book: their offices offer four acoustics zones for concentration, collaboration, communications and contemplation (see below and illustration).

Don't expect to get it all right immediately. Plantronics had a background sound masking system in every meeting room at first and it did indeed cover the noise levels coming in from other rooms. However, it also meant that people had to raise their voices to be heard within the rooms – the sound absorbers were absorbing the desired noises as well. They were switched off and the blocking of sounds from other rooms was sufficient.

In terms of other changes and lessons, Coffin explains that the cycle tends to happen in sevens. After seven days the individual wrinkles start to emerge – people needing chairs or desks adjusted, small stuff. After seven weeks they become departmental snags: more storage for an entire department, for example. After seven months, the enterprise-level trends emerge and people find out what's working and what isn't. Too much sound masking was one of the things emerging at the seven-month stage; the company added more of the soft walls throughout the building to cushion more noise including one 22m wall, which has graphics on the cushioning rather than on the walls as it had been before. Also, further sound damping has been added to the reception area. In many businesses, the reception area is actually one of the noisiest areas in the building; it is now a pleasant area to work in and to walk into, confirms Coffin.

The four acoustic C spaces

(from Myerson's *New Demographics, New Workspaces*)

Spaces to Concentrate:

Are not just necessary, but absolutely essential to offset an overdose of (poor) open plan workspaces.

Can be separate rooms, special booths or designated areas of the main office.

Eliminate noise and distractions.

Need strict working protocols for such spaces.

Are located away from noisy facilities such as kitchens, cafés, print rooms and social areas.

Feature adjustable ergonomic settings.

Have window views with natural light, connection to outside world.

Are equiped with audio masking technology and sound transformation systems.

Spaces to Collaborate:

Provide project space to spread out data, sheets, documentation.

Bring no worries about confidentiality or tidying away before project completion.

Can be reserved by the day, week or month.

Can adopt a character for a period of time, as project dictates.

Are studio-like: large surfaces, white boards, pens, digital image capture.

Have large visual walls and 'kitchen' tables.

Bring movable, flexible work settings.

Abolish department/function silos.

Feature dynamic and adjustable lighting to set the right ambience and mood.

Spaces to Contemplate:

Offer a break from work for sessions from 10 minutes to several hours.

Have domestic-like settings.

Allow recuperation from the stress and noise of main office.

Are quiet and enclosed, not the place for phone calls and loud conversations.

Have strong natural and organic elements, rich with plants, water.

Feature adjustable lighting, very distinct from core office.

Are above all quiet and enclosed.

Spaces to Communicate:

Have superb acoustic shielding for uninhibited energetic encounters.

Come in a mixture of face-to-face and virtual collaboration/communication.

Block outside noise and ensure privacy and confidentiality.

Come in a variety of 'walled' rooms and open spaces.

Each has its own set of requirements from the overall topology point of view but, most importantly it has an acoustic element. Following the guidelines established above, it's possible – without doors, thus saving on the cost of real estate – to build individual cells for head-down concentration time, meeting rooms with good sound insulation for communication and collaboration, and quiet areas for contemplation, often without walls and doors as Plantronics has done. The illustration below shows how Plantronics implemented the four acoustic zones.

WORK SPACE ZONES
FOR PRODUCTIVE INFORMATION WORK

CONCENTRATE

- Focused individual work
- Quiet enclosed space
- Private

COLLABORATE

- Group discussions
- Presentations
- Audio/video conferencing
- Brainstorming sessions
- Formal meeting area
- Stimulating

CONTEMPLATE

- Take time out
- Comfortable
- Re-energizing

COMMUNICATE

- Mixture of face-to-face and virtual collaboration / communication
- Superb acoustic sheilding
- Fixed or flexile desk dpace

Source: *New Demographics, New Workplaces* Jeremy Myerson et al

The impetus for these space moves has to come from the top of a business down and it is essential that either the company culture moves to adjust to them or that the company ethos is in the right place already.

There are some easy tricks to put into place to help mask noise. Some of these are in the British Association of Interior Specialists' *A Guide to Office Acoustics*.

Circular meeting pods are popular in business and are often made of glass; in order to avoid excessive noise make sure they are carpeted and have a mineral fibre ceiling to avoid reverberation.

Remember there are two types of acoustic control; absorption to deal with reverberation within a space and insulation, which deals with transferring noise from one area to another. It's important to judge which sort you're dealing with when designing spaces for each of your tasks.

Whatever you do about noise in your organization – and the authors urge you to take it seriously as an issue – do check your minimum requirements by law. Laws change so we're not going to rehash what's current in this book, but offices are usually exempt from regulations on noise at work. If you're concerned, check www.hse.gov.uk in the UK and its equivalents elsewhere in the world, but always aim to outperform the minimum requirement – your workforce will push themselves harder as a result.

Assess your workspace

Before you start, though – before putting any plan into place for changing your workspace around – let's consider the workforce. What sort of working space do they actually want?

This isn't a trivial question and it's not one that should be overlooked – but it's peculiar because it's what many managers actually do. They forget all about consulting the colleagues who will be working within it, or working around it. Recent corporate history is littered with companies that put together some sort of impromptu Gallup-style poll about employee satisfaction in general. This is a powerful tool but something more specific is necessary if you're going to put any serious investment into reshaping a working space.

All of this was part of the rationale behind the Leesman Index created by Annie Leeson and Tim Oldman, co-founders of Leesman.com (from LEESon and OldMAN). Launched in 2010, the index has a good claim to be the first genuinely independent workplace satisfaction tool. Indeed one of your authors, Philip, is on the advisory board.

Using web technology, the Leesman Index asks associates to rank and weight activities and put together a score for work environment satisfaction. The index takes buildings and workforce demographics into account and produces activity overviews as well as a snapshot of worker satisfaction. This can be related directly to productivity: more on this in a later chapter.

Note, however, that although this schema refers to management of workspaces specifically, the workspace does not have to be a traditional office premise in particular.

Leesman workspace satisfaction audit

Leesman is the leader in measuring the effectiveness of corporate workplaces and the Leesman Index benchmark is generated from the largest contemporary database of workplace satisfaction surveys available. It offers easy access to vital, empirical evidence to inform the design and management of commercial office environments. Its survey and analytics tools provide an inexpensive and systematic approach to the collection, analysis and benchmarking of workplace satisfaction data and generate a single, universal measure of effectiveness – the 'Lmi'.

MY WORKPLACE ENABLES ME TO WORK PRODUCTIVELY

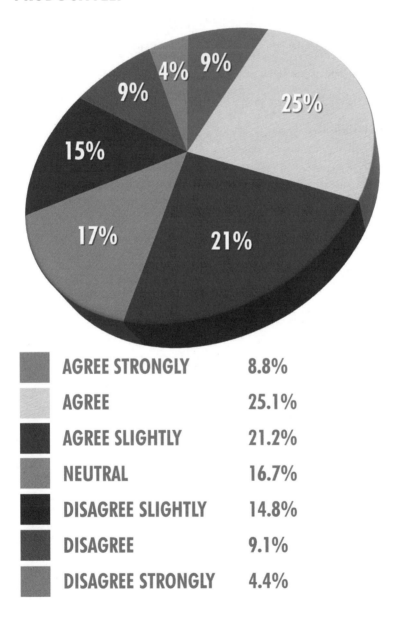

	AGREE STRONGLY	8.8%
	AGREE	25.1%
	AGREE SLIGHTLY	21.2%
	NEUTRAL	16.7%
	DISAGREE SLIGHTLY	14.8%
	DISAGREE	9.1%
	DISAGREE STRONGLY	4.4%

MY WORKPLACE IS A PLACE I'M PROUD TO BRING VISITORS TO

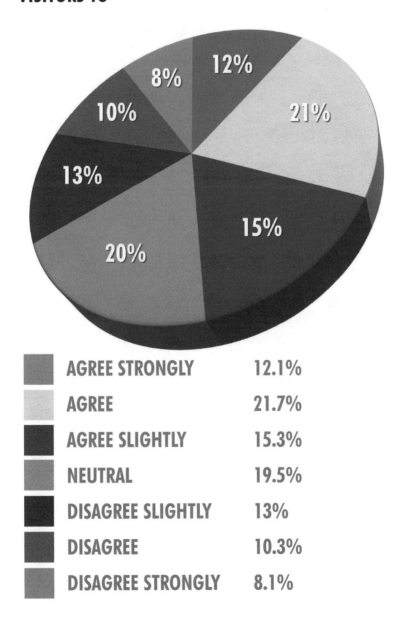

	AGREE STRONGLY	12.1%
	AGREE	21.7%
	AGREE SLIGHTLY	15.3%
	NEUTRAL	19.5%
	DISAGREE SLIGHTLY	13%
	DISAGREE	10.3%
	DISAGREE STRONGLY	8.1%

THE DESIGN OF MY WORKSPACE IS IMPORTANT TO ME

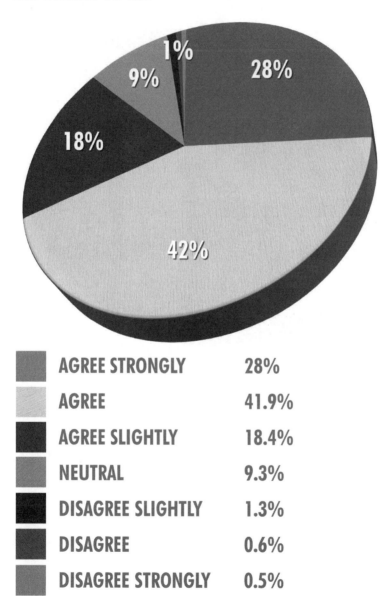

■	AGREE STRONGLY	28%
■	AGREE	41.9%
■	AGREE SLIGHTLY	18.4%
■	NEUTRAL	9.3%
■	DISAGREE SLIGHTLY	1.3%
■	DISAGREE	0.6%
■	DISAGREE STRONGLY	0.5%

MY WORKPLACE CREATES AN ENJOYABLE ENVIRONMENT TO WORK IN

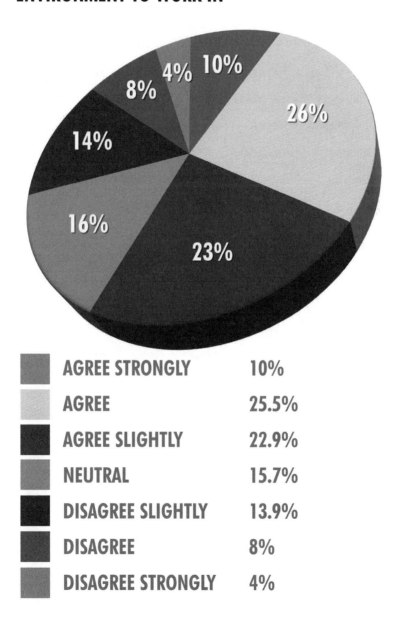

	AGREE STRONGLY	10%
	AGREE	25.5%
	AGREE SLIGHTLY	22.9%
	NEUTRAL	15.7%
	DISAGREE SLIGHTLY	13.9%
	DISAGREE	8%
	DISAGREE STRONGLY	4%

The survey

Questions focus on four main areas. The first determines which work activities are important to employees and how well these are supported by the workplace. Next, it examines satisfaction with the important physical features and facilities services of the office environment. Lastly, it probes the impact of workplace design on corporate image and culture, sense of pride, enjoyment, community and productivity at work.

Information is gathered via a confidential online questionnaire, which takes employees on average 11 minutes to complete. The survey uses a standardised core of simple, easily understood questions that do not vary and an optional array of additional, flexible modules. This gives organizations and their consultants the unrivalled ability to compare their results with thousands of others and, at the same time, collect detailed and insightful diagnostic data. The data is then housed in a powerful online environment called Leesman Analytics.

New types of workspace

Earlier in this chapter we referred to the various different forms of workspace in common use. Historically these have been valid. However, the authors of this book tend to think of three distinct workspace environments that may be more useful in the 21st century.

The smarter office or factory, or wherever someone actually works as their designated working place. It doesn't matter particularly which sort of office they have as long as it gets divided into the right sort of acoustic zones and as long as people can perform the appropriate tasks in the best manner.

The home: for the dispersed worker or home-worker, it goes without saying (but we'll say it anyway) that the home needs assessing for working just as any other workspace might. Once again this means starting from the task and moving from there. Is it the right place to perform the task? Is it adequate as a workspace, and is the person performing the task the right person to be working remotely?

In elsewhere space: this is the one people miss. The meeting in the coffee shop. The ad hoc workplace. The shared working space. There are many start-up spaces like this, from the aforementioned executive shared spaces in London's Canary

Wharf to the most basic start-ups with a bit of WiFi, a desk and that's about it.

All of these will be appropriate at different times and, for the last one, at different stages of a company's development. The rough and ready, inexpensive working space will suit a start-up, for example, whereas the more professional environment might suit someone wanting to take clients somewhere a little 'swish'.

On the next few pages is an overview of many space types to choose from: what they are typically used for, who likes working in them, pitfalls to avoid and recommendations to make the most of them.

NEW TYPES OF SPACE

OFFICES

QUIET ROOMS small enclosed spaces with acoustic privacy

QUIET AREAS comfortable and attractive, multiple work settings for individuals, low noise policy

COLLABORATION AREAS comfortable and adaptable for group needs, located away from quiet areas

SOCIAL HUBS relaxing 'off-stage' spaces with refreshments, for groups or individuals

ELSEWHERE

INSPIRING SPACES stimulating environments such as art galleries, museums or outdoor locations

NEUTRAL GROUND somewhere to hold meetings outside the corporate territory

TRANSITION SPACES public spaces used while in transit, including cafes and transport

HOME

HOME OR HOTEL ROOM somewhere private, peaceful and comfortable

QUIET ROOMS

WORK ACTIVITIES	PERSONAL STYLE
Short time slot Detailed, process work (e.g. data analysis) Confidential conversations Phone calls Unplanned focus required Short, private 1:1s	Needs peace and quiet Ideas will come from me, not outside I might need support/input from others at some point
POTENTIAL PITFALLS TO AVOID	MAKING THE MOST OF IT
These often aren't comfortable for long periods of time People can see you are having a private call/meeting Don't treat it like a private office	Use these rooms for 'unplanned' focused work, or book in advance Sit sideways to the door, not with your back to it Make it clear that you don't want interruptions

QUIET AREAS

WORK ACTIVITIES	PERSONAL STYLE
Time frame longer than acceptable for quiet room use Reading Deep thinking Detailed, focused work	Need peace and quiet to concentrate I might need support/input from others at some point Need space to think comfortably
POTENTIAL PITFALLS TO AVOID	**MAKING THE MOST OF IT**
These areas don't offer 'privacy' as such Some people may still come and find you/interrupt you Collaboration with others can disturb those working around you	This could be at your desk in open plan if you have a quiet environment Bring all the materials you need and get comfortable so that you can focus for longer

COLLABORATION AREAS / TEAM ROOMS

WORK ACTIVITIES	PERSONAL STYLE
Formally planned group activities Nucleus for project team and materials	Working with others Requiring absorption in 'project'

POTENTIAL PITFALLS TO AVOID	MAKING THE MOST OF IT
Ensure adequate separation from quiet areas where individuals are trying to focus	If possible, rearrange furniture etc to create the best set-up for the team Use physical artefacts, graphics, samples etc to build a shared mental model of the work among the team

SOCIAL HUB

WORK ACTIVITIES	PERSONAL STYLE
Informal meetings Relaxing with colleagues Non-work meetings Work that requires little concentration Takng a break	Prefer to be with others Like a buzzing environment
POTENTIAL PITFALLS TO AVOID	**MAKING THE MOST OF IT**
Not very effective as an overflow space for individual focused work	Allow it to be noisy Some offices ban explicity work focused meetings to ensure others can relax and socialise These spaces work best when they are genuinely 'off stage' and informal - location and design very important

INSPIRING SPACES

WORK ACTIVITIES	PERSONAL STYLE
Creative work Team-building Thinking time Focused individual work	Changing environment changes state of mind Looking for stimulus from outside as well as from me

POTENTIAL PITFALLS TO AVOID	MAKING THE MOST OF IT
Few inspiring places cater for people to work in for any length of time	Make sure the work facilities actually suport what you need to do, or you bring everything you need If possible, keep it simple: a pad, a pencil and your thoughts

NEUTRAL GROUND

WORK ACTIVITIES

Informal meetings

Meetings with clients or third parties

Semi-engaging individual work

Externally inspired, individual work

PERSONAL STYLE

Looking for a change of scenery

Want 'non-corporate' backdrop to meet in

Want 'anonymity' rather than 'privacy'

POTENTIAL PITFALLS TO AVOID

Not ideal for confidential meetings or work

Strangers coming and going can make it hard to stake and maintain territory

MAKING THE MOST OF IT

Choose locations to be memorable for important meetings

Create your own bubble in which to work and enjoy activity around you without being distracted by it

Use the background hubbub to mask your own conversations

TRANSITION SPACES

WORK ACTIVITIES	PERSONAL STYLE
Checking emails Making phone calls Reading Only simple work tools required Deep thinking	Able to shut off from external distractions Able to do the tasks without great focus

POTENTIAL PITFALLS TO AVOID	MAKING THE MOST OF IT
Little audio privacy for confidential conversations Take care not to disturb other people Focused work can require some discipline/absorption in the work	Time - just enough to cover a few small tasks? Or long enough to absorb yourself in your thoughts? Space - find a spot with the least disruption from people traffic Alternatively, take advantage of this time to switch off and relax

HOME OR HOTEL ROOM

WORK ACTIVITIES	PERSONAL STYLE
Deep, focused work Thinking, problem-solving New thinking Routine work that takes time and focus but not challenging thinking	Want to work alone on this - it's challenging Happy to work alone on this - it's easy Don't need discipline to do this (very engaging or have a deadline etc.)
POTENTIAL PITFALLS TO AVOID	MAKING THE MOST OF IT
Challenging work requires confidence to tackle in isolation Low social interaction may not suit Environment must be clear of other distractions (dogs, children etc.) Dull work can require external motivations, e.g. deadlines	Separate 'home' and 'work' items and tasks as far as possible Make yourself comfortable - you can .be free from office norms Separate and organise your tasks, take breaks in between

Source: *Work Topology - Practical Guide for the Simply Smarter Office*, Plantronics

THE **SMARTER WORKING** MANIFESTO

What's essential is that the task and the person plus the surrounding people are considered well in advance of the place. The right working space might emerge as a simple result of contemplating what has to be done rather than proscribing where it should be before even thinking about the job at hand.

Points to note for managers:

> You need to survey your workers and find out what is likely to work best – trusting to instinct is never scientific.

> Actionable, precise findings are essential in every case. The Leesman Index offers just such actionable input for all three of the core disciplines – space, IT and HR.

> An audit isn't complete once it's done – it needs revisiting frequently. Often what people thought would work for them doesn't deliver and they need to look at something else or suggest alternatives.

Your workspace, your brand

Our final section of this chapter is about your organization and its culture overall and how you reflect this in your workspace. The space will become identified with working for you by your colleagues and employees; it will speak to visitors about the values you espouse. Earlier in this chapter we mentioned the reception area with the car parked in the middle – that's the sort of thing we're talking about. Are you a strictly corporate, regimented company? Are you self-consciously wacky, as a handful are?

During Plantronics' upgrade to its current premises, Tim Oldman, acting as a consultant, was very clear: a good workspace needs to be enjoyed by associates, customers, partners and the wider stakeholder community around it. This will have an impact on corporate social responsibility as much as working practices themselves.

Tim's suggestion was that Plantronics should adopt acoustics as its theme as it was and is an acoustics business. For readers who don't know, the company's pedigree was as a supplier of headsets but it has gone beyond that into the smart management of sound through speakerphones and related products. Oldman hit on the idea of making the whole new premises about the management of sound: an acoustic temple.

The marketing team coined the term 'acoustic intelligence' to describe the need for an understanding of space, telecommunications and human acoustics. The office itself is arguably a laboratory for how voice can be made intelligible and unintelligible by turn where it needs to, and the impact of speech. Audio ergonomics has become a major feature of the Plantronics office.

It is at this point that the workplace starts to take on a character of its own. This book's authors have seen a number of approaches, some of which are extreme, to workplace activities and, indeed, designs:

A kitchen to make coffee or other refreshments is a given. In some instances a business insists on providing free food for employees. In a number of companies it is commonplace for people to come in before breakfast and help themselves to cereal offerings on the spot. If they were 'early morning people' and at their best straight after breakfast, that's when the company wanted them to work.

Naming of meeting rooms is often a means of adding a bit of fun to an organization. One of the authors has been to two fairly ordinary-looking open plan offices in recent years that have had meeting rooms named after the James Bond films. Each no doubt thinks they're unique.

Childcare in the workplace has been experimented with on many occasions. In the 1980s, there was a spate of companies proud of the fact that they had an on-site crèche for their staff. These experiments proved short-lived, however, as working parents soon decided they would rather leave the children with local childcare than take them on a commute at both ends of the day.

The counter-argument

For some people, this is going to be a load of old hooey.

Here are a few things that can go wrong with an environment in which people work remotely. We will deal with specific management techniques to get around them in a later chapter, but they are worth outlining in brief:

- Staff don't always perceive someone to be working when they are not visible on site

- Staff don't always work when they are not visible on site

- Staff feel isolated

- Colleagues' homes may not be suitable as workplaces

- Exclusion from corporate culture

It is undoubtedly for this reason that a number of organizations have decided to instruct their employees to work on site and have abandoned flexible working completely. Surprisingly, two high profile examples are in the IT world; Yahoo! and Hewlett-Packard have both, within 18 months of each other, issued edicts suggesting that the best way to collaborate is face to face – missing the point that in companies of their size and geographical dispersion, face to face is rarely an option anyway.

The authors of this book believe these companies to be wrong, having seen smarter working work too many times.

Action points
for professionals

Understand your job's key activities and the spaces available to you in which to work. Perched at your desk may not be the most effective place for you to perform a task, even if it just means scheduling a meeting with a colleague in the canteen over a coffee instead of by one of your usual workstations. Understand yourself and where you perform a particular task well – do not assume the same place will suit you for each different task.

Seek out the different acoustic zones. They may have been formalized or they may not – find what works for you.

Build up your portfolio of working spaces and be aware of which tasks you do best.

Action points
for managers

Survey your colleagues on what they want and need from their office in terms of smarter working. Insist on complete buy-in to the survey; if you're planning a 'big bang' style office revamp, make it obvious to colleagues that they have to speak now or forfeit their say in how the business will run. Remember a survey needs to have distinct action points at the end of it so a lot of the 'are you happy?' type of surveys out there will be less than appropriate. The Leesman Index has been tried and tested by one of the authors of this book and we recommend it as a result; whatever you decide, make sure the questions will lead to solid actions.

Plan your new office. If it's your old office with a facelift, so be it. But plan it as if the workforce doesn't have to be there all the time, as we decided earlier. Plan so that everyone can sit in any seat and work out the money you've just saved. Consider abandoning landlines and their resulting costs.

Change your existing premises if you have that sort of authority. Look at activity-based workspaces and consider the four acoustic zones: contemplation, concentration, communication and collaboration. Put something in place to ensure all your professionals and visitors have somewhere suitable for their needs in your working space. If you're lucky enough to be commissioning a new building, be aware of all of those considerations and have the acoustic intelligence to work out how to make the building perform as part of your strategy.

Put metrics in place so that you can measure business results. These should include staff retention and consequent savings on recruitment, productivity (we do realize this can be difficult to measure exactly) and profitability as costs on desk space go down.

Put some of yourself into the office. Remember the Google example, Plantronics' paean to acoustics and even the OTT place with that blasted car in reception; all of these were statements about who the companies were and how they wanted to be perceived. Your office should be not only functional but a pleasure for the right employee to visit; they may work remotely but coming into base should feel like some sort of treat. There are side benefits too; at job interviews there will be self-selection as Mr or Ms Corporate Suit-and-Boot decide they won't want to work somewhere with bubble gum machines in reception, or indeed the other way around – someone who prefers jeans and sneakers will come to an obvious blue-chip environment and decide quite quickly that it isn't for them.

Chapter Two:

Going Virtual With Impact

TECHNOLOGY'S NOT ENOUGH

GEORGE STILL HADN'T QUITE GOT
THE HANG OF USING HIS VOICE PROPERLY

In this chapter you will learn:

- What technologies are available and what you'll need to master them.
- What the flexible worker actually needs.
- What the current state of technology in and out of the workplace is likely to deliver.

Technology's not enough

So, have you got all the technology you need for your colleagues to work virtually? Good. Think you've done it and are now covered for virtual working? Forget it. Unless you address the managerial issues of how to keep your colleagues impactful and creative, you've wasted your money.

Throughout Chapter One, we worked on the principle that readers would want to keep their office. The office is a hub, a base of operations. However, a lot of people now have the opportunity to work virtually – which actually means working, but working somewhere else.

Despite a number of organizations opting for the purely virtual model of working, we still think physical workspace is crucial for most businesses. There isn't any substitute for the buzz you'll get when telesales people are in the same room together and many people find that if they're out of the company's sight for any length of time their motivation starts to suffer and people lose focus. That is no way to run a business or public sector entity, obviously.

Nonetheless, an office is not always necessary. The reason is simple; we have arrived where we are through the development of technology. The mistake a lot of organizations make, however, is that they assume technology alone will carry them through. It's absolutely not just a matter of automating a few processes and giving people some nice new headsets – it's a complex piece of human re-engineering. As professionals embrace the newfound freedom of working dispersed, they often underestimate the constraints of virtual working.

Home-working for instance, relies heavily on written and voice communications – we meet less often face to face. The impact on our communication, our collaboration and our ability to engage our colleagues can be significant. New skills, tools and techniques are essential to ensure nothing is lost in translation between dispersed working individuals.

On the tools side, the goal is to provide high-fidelity equivalents of paper and face-to-face collaboration (co-authoring, whiteboarding) while providing the best possible voice interaction, with excellent voice intelligibility. Network bandwidth permitting, the nirvana of 3D virtual presence is then just around the corner, no?

Unfortunately, this wonderland isn't consistently available. Whereas wideband audio (hi-fidelity voice) is feasible in broadband networks, a lack of quality of service in data networks and background noise often upset a natural dialogue, undermining impactful communications and collaboration.

The inability to understand a remote colleague or a customer defeats the purpose of a virtual encounter and drops virtual collaboration engagement to sub-zero levels. Professional ICT functions need to go to great lengths to ensure equipment such as phones (fixed, softphone and mobile) and conference speakerphones are in good functioning shape, enhanced by accessories (headsets or extra microphones), in combination with high quality networks to ensure engagement levels are not compromised.

So, let's look in some more detail at what you actually need.

The ICT march

It's probably apocryphal but there's a popular story that quotes a senior VP of a major computer company in the 1950s as saying there may one day be a need for as many as five computers in the world. And one of them might have the need for as many as 64 megabytes of memory. Some versions say that was a telecoms company, others say it was a major typewriter manufacturer; personally, we think it was a drunken journalist one evening seeing how quickly it would become accepted fact if he made something like that up. Any paperwork proving definitively that someone actually said it has mysteriously disappeared – that at least must be true; it was on Wikipedia.

The point is that nobody ever thought we'd end up as computer-dependent as we are. Computers in the 1950s were great big scary things, some of which were quite useful in the industrial sector but most of which went crazy and tried to take over the world in 1960s TV and movies. Most of those were not actually real computers.

Real computers were doing things like calculations and going into making the Moonshot possible in 1969. Most computing was done on large mainframes with large spooling reel-to-reel tapes, dedicated to the accounts department. Number-crunching was their main function and the first hints that accounts departments would one day be automated emerged.

Spool forward to the 1970s and the first hint that people could have their own personal computers started to arrive. In the UK Sinclair and Amstrad did their pioneering work to forge what would become a home computing revolution and a decade later IBM came out with the Personal Computer, which we still call the PC although sales are finally falling in favour of tablets as we write (don't sniff at this – a lifetime of 35 years for a basic architecture that's still available is unprecedented in computing terms).

This is the stage at which computing became distributed, everyone had their own processing power on their desktop (for 'everyone' you need to read 'office-based knowledge workers'). People started accustoming themselves to the idea that a screen in the home and in the office was normal, although the laptop models we know today were prohibitively expensive.

Move forward a little more and the trend towards having everything on your own desktop computer has started to lose its gloss a little. There are good reasons for this. People getting viruses in their computers have discovered that putting all of the risk in a single place isn't clever or desirable. There are powerful arguments for putting things elsewhere. People's offices can burn down. People can lose data because of less dramatic user errors. More practically, people were starting to look to edit documents on different devices. You might log on and start a document at work. On going home, you may want to edit it further. In the 1980s and 1990s, you'd almost certainly have taken it home on disk.

This was fine unless someone else took the same thing home on another disk and worked on it. Then you're into 'multiple version syndrome', which is pretty much every creative person's nightmare. Jeanette has done an excellent job of updating a document but so has Bryan, who has taken it into another direction; meanwhile, Lars has started translating the original because he didn't realize the other two had started reworking it. Someone will have to assimilate all of the changes. This is woefully inefficient.

(Sidenote: sharp readers will by now be saying 'hang on, that's a problem with internal communications rather than the technology', and they'd be right. Smarter working is as much to do with using technology intelligently and appropriately as with owning the technology in the first place).

So a number of companies started offering something called ASP – application service provision. This involved storing data and indeed applications off-site; you'd log in and use someone else's server, and it didn't matter whether you were at home or in the office. Initially, this pretty much tanked; the five people in Europe who owned the right equipment to connect to a remote server rapidly grew tired of waiting for the remote system to respond to a command. As we moved into the 21st century, broadband started to become a little more widespread and this technique of using someone else's computer as your own – sometimes called virtualization if you were having your entire computer hosted, sometimes called hosting, sometimes called 'cloud' if you were having little bits hosted – started to take off. Google started to make it very popular indeed with the advent of Google Docs, which gave rise to the (minimally) paid-for Google Apps. You could now have an office suite in the cloud, writing and editing as you went, without any difficulty as long as your connection was robust.

Older commentators took to clicking their tongues and saying 'we were doing all this with mainframes ages ago'. Younger commentators pointed instead to the benefits not only of collaborating in real time on documents and projects, but also on how beneficial social media can be. Exchange views and get help, all in real time – what's to dislike?

Digitizing your workflow

We have to make a few assumptions when discussing what you actually need in terms of technology to make your working life smarter. For sure, it must be possible to work in multiple locations. This doesn't have to be all the time; a salesperson can work flexibly but it's understood that they will have to be in front of the customer rather than on the phone or email for much of the time. Actors are not well advised to phone their part in (although a few we could mention might as well). There are a lot of roles, however, that can be flexible a lot of the time. And they need technology. Here we look at some of the tools a business will need in order to keep track of a mobile workforce.

Electronic substitutes for manual processes in business have been happening since the late 1970s or early 1980s, it's just that we've only recently started identifying them as such. Being able to walk to an ATM and use a combination of cards and codes instead of going into a bank and writing yourself a cheque to get some cash, means you've been using an elementary form of business process automation. It's a term that gets used a lot but it doesn't actually mean anything very complicated every time.

Automation in office communication can happen in much the same way. You need two foundations: a directory of contacts that can show presence (a combination of being online with an indication of preparedness/readiness to communicate) together with a real-time calendaring system.

A rock-solid shared calendar system is a must for the smallest microbusiness or the largest corporation, but the simple practicalities have to come first. If you can't lean over to someone's desk and say 'are you free for a meeting tomorrow, Dave?' you have to be able to find that out through automation. There are numerous inexpensive alternatives available, starting from Google Apps and moving to the most sophisticated corporate workflow system.

You will also come to depend on 'electronic presence', normally called just 'presence', through which your colleagues inside and outside the business know whether you are at your desk (wherever 'at your desk' might mean in this instance – it might be more useful to call it 'available').

Beyond that, there are a number of communication 'gears' that make dispersed working productive:

1st gear: instant messaging, where you have (near instant) asynchronous communications: the next generation of SMS. If someone is at their computer (or smartphone or tablet) and logged on, they will show as present in the system. Remember to switch this off when, say, someone else is using your laptop for a presentation.

2nd gear: telephony; no matter whether you're using vintage/analogue, digital (Voice Over IP) or mobile telephony, you can call someone. The world has never had so many devices we can phone with. This is where some extra finessing can be useful through the use of headsets that connect to multiple devices. A single headset can link to a softphone on the computer through Bluetooth or USB, as well as Bluetoothing to a mobile phone and connecting to a landline where these are still in use. Calibrate the system correctly and the deskphone or softphone will show as busy when you're on a mobile call. The usefulness is clear; the user doesn't have to switch manually between lines depending on whether they're on Skype, Microsoft Lync, a mobile call or a landline call.

3rd gear: multi-party telephony or audio conferencing. This used to be complex but it isn't now, at least not to the user. Technically it is, of course, a little more difficult. There are numerous options, from corporate party lines to consumer/small business products such as Powwownow.co.uk or GoToMeeting. Just log into the site, enter your email address and you'll be given a number and an access code. Share it between callers and if you all dial it, you're conference-calling very easily. This can eliminate the need for short meetings and indeed meetings where travel would be prohibitively expensive.

4th gear: video telephony and its multi-party equivalent video conferencing. Once again, formerly the province of the technologist and now available to anyone with a smartphone or a tablet, this is a convenient way to avoid unnecessary travel time to short meetings and to make a day more productive.

5th gear (or overdrive) is the high definition telepresence: as above but in high definition. A number of refinements are available or in development; author Guy saw 3D teleconferencing demonstrated as early as

2006 and it was very good; only about one-third of the people in the room suffered motion sickness. This will improve as technologies develop. Businesses including Polycom and others offer life-sized video conferencing.

Unified communications and collaboration

There are two sides to this sort of collaboration. One is a consumer/small business led piece, called social networking or social media. The second is the enterprise scale stuff, known as unified communications and collaboration. Definitions for each can be pretty fluid. Let's start with the latter.

Enterprise UC&C

Industrial-strength-style unified communications and collaboration – often called UC or UC&C by the people selling it and those in technical support – is an extension of what used to be called unified messaging. This took faxes, voicemails and emails and sent them straight to people's inboxes rather than to the fax machine, the mobile handset or any individual piece of technology. This was a good idea but limited in two ways:

1. It was static and non-interactive. Guy sends Philip a text, email, fax, voicemail, Philip picks it up and then responds – the message itself is inert, it's more akin to emailing than speaking.

2. Obviously, it would be limited to delivery to Philip's inbox. Mostly, this would be using Microsoft Outlook, which might need add-ons to ensure its compatibility with whichever medium the message was in, but primarily it would be desktop computer or, later, laptop-based.

Unified communications started to improve on this from around 2005 by eliminating both of those limitations. It would become easy not just to send a message but to start a conversation using different media.

Let's take a theoretical example before launching into a couple of real case studies of how this works by getting back to the co-authors of this book, Philip and Guy, who live in different countries. Guy has a concern about a section of the book being written so he IMs Philip. Guy is at his desktop in London, Philip is carrying his phone in the Netherlands. Philip answers Guy through a 3G or 4G connection but it becomes apparent they need to speak. Philip therefore picks up his mobile phone and, using Skype – he might have used

Plantronics' internal Microsoft Lync system had Guy been an employee – they speak, either through video or audio. Eventually, Philip realizes Guy needs to see something to understand, so using Skype's paid-for, professional service, he transfers the video call to his laptop and shares his screen with Guy.

None of this is difficult but we've just walked through escalating a contact from IM (instant message) – pretty much an updated version of texting a mobile – to call, video-call and screen-sharing.

Meanwhile, Guy wants someone else's perspective so he tries to contact Luis, whom you will meet later in this chapter. He sees that Luis is unavailable but – and this is where Luis' use of social media structures is clever – by searching his social media stream, Guy can see whether Luis has answered the question before. Or perhaps one of his colleagues will see the query and answer it in his absence.

You can, we hope, see that physical presence in the office becomes a much less important issue than it was before.

Unified Communications recently has expanded to include collaboration, with companies such as MindLink offering a console of incoming communications, through email, social networks (public) and company social network lookalikes.

The idea is to have a continuum of communications coming in and out.

Corporate businesses generally have to decide which form of UC they will adopt.

Social networking

It would be wrong to write off social networking and unified communications as two different things – we're doing it in this book for convenience rather than for anything else. Social media has become part of unified communications and collaborations, but is more common in the small business arena.

Most readers – if not all – will already be familiar with Facebook, Google+, LinkedIn, Twitter and the various other social networks that are out there. Some may even have read author Guy's books on the subject, *This Is Social Media* and *This Is Social Commerce*.

There are many applications for social media in business. IBM knowledge management evangelist Luis Suarez, based in Spain but working internationally, uses it as a preferred medium and has cut out 97% of his email as a result.

Case Study:
Luis doesn't like email

Suarez started on his email-free journey when he realized that every time he came back from holiday it took him two days to catch up with all of the communications lying in wait for him. Clearly, this wasn't an appropriate way to communicate in business. He also noted that people were emailing him with an issue while he was on holiday and by the time he was back the problem was solved, but he still had to plough through all of his communications to find this out.

Simultaneously, as someone senior within IBM, he found himself approached by students to help with dissertations. The incoming generation, however, were not using email to get in touch. "They found me through my blog and it hit me – in talking to them over the last eight or nine years, I never used email." Skype yes, Twitter, LinkedIn and other networks by all means, but the incoming generation (and if they were incoming a decade ago they're well established in the workplace now) don't use email. It felt natural not to as well.

Even more importantly, he felt email had fallen into disrepute through abuse. It had long since ceased to be the best way to communicate with people. There was a lot of CCing people into emails purely for tit-for-tat company politics that would hit productivity; it was used as a delegation machine as well, plus it was too useful for people justifying their work.

He therefore stopped using email and used himself as a guinea pig. Note that he was senior enough to make this work; he was able to challenge the way people worked rather than have to fit around them.

Social media connections, whether on a corporate system such as IBM's closed systems or LinkedIn (for example), offer several advantages over email:

Everyone can see what you're saying unless you use private messaging – and if you switch to 'private' it is more difficult to send attachments, or delegate, or send invitations or add do-lists. It's focused and restricted and needs to reach the point.

You can click through and find who is contacting you and by extension why they might want to do so.

It prevents working in silos; everything is shared, it forces collaboration.

People have to take care over what they say; everything will add to their reputation.

People will know you're away and step in and help when a query to which they know the answer crops up.

Suarez points out that some companies block large attachments or give people a 'mail jail' ceiling for the amount of large attachments they may receive and the sender doesn't find out until later – so if a supplier sends, say, a large attachment by email, it may not arrive.

Other people

There are learning issues for people wanting to take up this form of communication. Suarez says you need resilience; when he started it was a one-person movement and now it is a thousands-strong idea. Suarez believes social structures are more constructive and productive than the older styles, which is why he advocates them.

Better emails

Inevitably, as an evangelist Suarez is very persuasive. His own life has improved dramatically because of the reduction in email he receives. Much of what he does and says is wrong with email is because of the way people use it; there are also good reasons for continuing with it but using it better:

Suppliers and customers: not everybody is as influential as a senior person within IBM. If a small business or freelance wants to communicate in a smart fashion then that means contacting clients in whichever way they demand. If you won't communicate by email then a number of organizations will soon find someone who will.

Peer pressure: granted, there appears to be a generation moving away from email but we're in transition right now: it isn't dead. Transition means not moving right away from it just yet.

The authors would certainly advocate better use of email than is prevalent in a number of organizations, however. Bad practices to stamp out would include:

Cluttering work emails with private messages. Most people carry a smartphone that should be capable of receiving private as well as business messages – use it!

CYA or 'cover your anatomy'. Emails sent with a view to making yourself look good or cover a mistake are never productive.

Endless newsletters. Many people sign up for newsletters with every intention of reading them but they stop getting around to it very quickly. Resign from them – if the authors have failed to arouse your interest, that's not your problem, it's theirs.

There are numerous applications for social media. Digital footprints are so important now that research organizations including Gartner actually refer to companies having a 'digital edge' (see *The Digital Edge*, McDonald and Rowsell-Jones). This isn't a bland reference to some sort of nebulous 'marketing edge' but the belief that the physical edge, the borders of a company, have moved in the light of the digital world. This adds value, the authors believe, by adding access to the company at different points, and disrupting existing business models.

Research by author Guy in *This Is Social Commerce* echoes the point. People are using social technologies in recruitment and reaching new employees, they are reaching new customers, promoting, researching and developing. Miss it at your peril.

Which social media?

There are two ways of deploying social media in your organization. One is through the cloud, using someone else's server and indeed a branded system of some sort. The other is to go for something more proprietary.

The public option

Facebook, LinkedIn, Google+ and many other social media networks offer closed or private groups for people wanting to communicate in that way. There are many reasons this can be a good idea for the smaller enterprise:

Cost – most of these are free at the point of entry. Paid-for versions of LinkedIn come with extra functionality.

Ease: many people will already be familiar with the interfaces.

Google+ comes with hangouts so can be used for video meetings as well as exchanging emails. It's a remarkable system for a low cost.

Among the disadvantages might be:

Privacy: nobody is suggesting Facebook or LinkedIn will change their privacy options anytime soon (although do read which rights you're assigning them when you upload pictures and content).

Leaks: it's very easy to be on LinkedIn and Facebook and simply forget that you've read something in what ought to be a private forum then reproduce it for anyone interested to read. There are frequent complaints on

Facebook that privacy has been breached; usually this is nothing to do with the network itself but a user's error.

The semi-public option

Podio, Jive, the Microsoft-owned Yammer, Cisco's Jabber and others offer Facebook-like services that are not available to people outside your organization or group.

Advantages:

Familiar interface

Everything Suarez points to as an advantage to a social collaboration model

Sharing of documents and links is easy

Disadvantages:

Rightly or wrongly, some people reject these networks on the grounds that they are 'yet another thing to follow', partly because they are overloaded by other people using their existing communications tools badly but that is the reality of it and it's not going away.

For this category and the public version, you're permanently in someone else's playground and not paying for it. This gives them the right to move the goalposts, change the rules, whatever they want to do. They probably won't – but it's not your space on the web, it's someone else's. And they can do what they wish with it.

The backbone infrastructure

For business workflow automation and unified communications and collaboration to happen, clearly pieces of core software and hardware are needed.

Dispersed working must be underpinned with the right operating environment for collaboration – a software as well as hardware infrastructure that will serve video, whiteboarding and every other conceivable element of unified communications. Microsoft Lync is an excellent example, as is Cisco's rival system Jabber – others may emerge in future. Watch the market and find the best and most technically elegant 'glue' to hold your business together when it is geographically dispersed – and keep it up to date.

Video cameras on and beyond every client device, possibly even a video room for extended time conferencing. To look professional it's not safe to assume that the camera built into the computer or smartphone will do the trick; if the device is handheld there will be a lot of shake and eye lines can be badly misaligned.

Servers and networking infrastructure with good bandwidth for throughput of video in multiple channels. Video is bandwidth-hungry and colleagues wanting to use it to chat need immediate access.

Security – this is a given. Let's accept that 'impregnable' does not exist; your systems must be as close as they can get.

Virtual private network (VPN) - Smarter Working is only feasible if remote associates have access to all the information and applications needed to do their jobs. A major concern for managers is of course that such access can be done in a most secure fashion. VPNs provide a secure tunnel to shared drives, enterprise applications like order-entry, purchasing, personnel records etc. An operations professional not being able to access his Oracle or SAP systems would make smarter working impossible. An added benefit is that VPN also allows your IT team to provide remote support to your PC; the smarter worker grants them access, the IT team 'takes over' the computer for a little while and soon your PC will be fixed, tuned for the next many hours of peaceful and productive virtual work.

Networks: the Achilles heel

Of course, a number of readers will look at the discussions between Guy and Philip in the above illustrations and start to wonder just what planet we're on. In the commercial world, where networks are often robust, it works. It just does. Philip is going to have no problem.

What's actually likely to happen, however, is that Guy logs on to Skype to speak to Philip and then notices that although they can hear each other, only one can see the other. Both have their cameras switched on correctly but no video is reaching Guy, so they decide to make do and just speak. Until Philip appears to stop. Guy, imagining it's his turn to speak, starts but doesn't get a reply. He still has full WiFi bars on his screen so just in case, he tries opening a web page… and realizes that although his internal network at home is fine, he hasn't been getting through to the outside world for a while.

He restarts his router. They contact each other again until the internet freezes up on them once more. Eventually, and reluctantly given the nature of the book being written, they concede they'll be better off on the phone. Or carrier pigeon.

The reality of unified communication and collaboration is that it works well only in an environment in which there is a good, reliable internet connection. In the UK, this means there are areas that suffer because they are too far from the exchange and they are still using old copper cabling, so the signal degrades. If you are aiming to use flexible working as a means of moving your business forward then part of your audit of your employees' workspaces must include something on connectivity – 4G may not be along quickly enough to get everyone as connected as you'd like. Much of the problem – and employers need to address this – is that employees are under the impression that their domestic broadband set-ups will do. They won't, for the following reasons:

If it goes wrong it isn't prioritized in the same way as a business broadband set-up would be.

Mostly it's based on what's called 'contested' lines. This means that during the day when the neighbours are out, you'll get a big bit of broadband all to yourself. It will feel very quick and the quality will be excellent. When the neighbours are back in the evening they will be using it too, with their own login and password; it's secure, but sharing the same 'pipe'.

Think of it like a water supply; everyone turns their taps on and the water pressure, therefore the quality of the service, plummets. Except that with tablet computers, game consoles, smart TVs and smartphones as well as computers it's more like everyone turning all of their taps on at once. No exceptions.

There is very little comeback because the companies will tell you that you should have had business grade internet in the first place. This means when it goes wrong you're prioritized and there are minimum speed service levels for up and download speed, jitter and latency. The agreed levels of service are called the service level agreement. You need to understand what's in this and what comeback you have if it's not reached.

HD voice

It is at this point that the authors are going to sound a little like middle-aged gents lamenting the state of the modern youth but, it has to be said, there are areas in which people are no longer as skilled as previous generations in business. One of these is in using their voices to communicate.

Previous generations had little choice. They would send a memo and it would take a day to get around – pick up the phone and someone would be on the end, reliably, and you could speak to them and get something arranged. The array of alternatives now on offer have made this less of an automatic option, and the quality of the voice offerings often militates against this being the ideal medium through which to communicate.

This is because the typical landline phone of yore would be based on narrowband technology. It would use less of the sonic spectrum available – communications were fine in short bursts but longer phone calls were wearing. Now we have wideband sound (or high definition voice) available; it carries less distortion and more nuances.

It's a more impactful means of communicating than the rather dry written word but meanwhile an incoming generation has the phone as its least favourite means of communication. It's becoming essential to relearn the voice as an essential tool for communication – the prevalence of voice over internet orotocol (VoIP) means the next generation will be using its HD power more. So we could end up with a new generation of people who have excluded themselves – with the forty-pluses and twenty-somethings voice-literate while the thirty-somethings struggle.

But HD voice is far from standard fare (yet). It will take all elements of the communications food chain to embed it: fixed and mobile networks, communications software, handsets and headsets – with a promise of quality of service.

The flexible worker's toolkit

The seed of this book was sown in the 1980s. It became possible – expensively and with great physical effort – to carry around a mobile phone (heavy at the time and only used for calling: texting hadn't happened yet) and a laptop computer (at the time these were unsuitable for putting on your lap because they weighed rather a lot). This meant it was perfectly feasible to carry around everything necessary for many jobs and yet people were stuck with turning up at offices after an uncomfortable commute every day.

Here, then, is a list of items currently available to the mobile worker – which should be provided either on a 'bring your own device' (BYOD – covered later in this chapter) basis or supplied by your company. We will look into some pros and cons of these at the end of this chapter.

Mobile phone: preferably a smartphone. Business people will benefit from suitable apps, configuring their own handheld system. It is possible to design enterprise apps as well.

Headset: a decent earpiece, headset or other wearable is essential for isolating noise from the phone both for the speaker and the listener. Many companies offer excellent models and, yes, the cheaper they are the less likely they are to do a job. Many will pick up a call simply by being lifted from a desk; some will communicate with the desktop computer to tell it the user is on the phone so that people don't try to IM or call when they are busy.

Should you be genuinely desk-bound there are excellent microphones available that sit on the desktop and offer high quality audio for podcasting, webinars etc. The Blue Snowball and Blue Yeti, for example, offer broadcast-quality sound and the Yeti has an earphone socket.

A computer: laptop, netbook, desktop, tablet – depending on the other tasks a user has to perform, the exact nature of the computer is not important.

Backed by the infrastructure described above, these should be all you need to be a fairly decent mobile worker. Check your headset for Microsoft Lync, Cisco Jabber or other UCC certification.

Crucially, none of these require an actual office premises in which to reside.

Service provision
– is it adequate?

There are two ways of having your IT requirements serviced: do it yourself or outsource it. The decision, which for many readers will already have been taken, may depend on the size of your organization and your inclination to become IT infrastructure experts rather than focus on what you do for a living.

Regardless, there are a number of questions you need to consider when talking to your technology provider, whether internally or externally:

1. Should we move to the cloud? The cloud is a matter of using someone else's computer systems rather than your own and can be a very good idea, with your own technology acting as a terminal. Done correctly, this will look and feel as though you are using your own systems. Don't forget to ask, though:

> What happens about backup? Many companies assume that they're automatically backed up if they're using cloud technology. They may not be; if there's only one copy of your work in the cloud and your hosting company has a problem then you still have a problem.

Ask what your cloud provider is doing to ensure this never becomes a crisis.

Where, physically, is your data? And, more particularly, is it being stored to your own country's data protection standards (which will be enforceable by law) or to the one in the host territory? One business Guy spoke to once had its data stored in India. It was fine until they asked: 'Are you compliant with the Data Protection Act in the UK?' And the polite and entirely reasonable answer came back: 'We're not even in the same continent, why would we be?'

Ask about security. Data centres – the places in which your data will be stored – may have machinegun nests (probably not literally), fire-proofing, all sorts of security behind them. Go for a bargain basement cost and you may find your data – for which you are legally responsible – is actually in someone's basement. Always ask.

2. Which form of UC&C would you recommend? At the moment, this is likely to be a contest between Microsoft and Cisco – and could well be a choice of items 'because that's what your supplier sells'. Ask about reasons for recommendations, always.

3. What is the service level agreement? You may or may not consider you need to pay for 24-hour phone support. If you opt for 'office hours only' then don't forget that if your server goes down at 5.05 pm on Friday you won't be supported until 9 am the following Monday.

BYOD, BYOA ... BYOC?

It is also worth considering your stance on BYOD or BYOA (bring your own app) but beware of BYOC, which we'll cover later in this section. The proliferation of smartphones and tablets throughout the developed world can mean there is no need to duplicate someone's device in the workplace. They may have a perfectly good device through which they can communicate. Why give someone a company iPhone or Android when they have a suitable widget in their pocket already?

There are a number of issues you need to address before deciding what to do about BYOD:

Which devices will you support? The temptation is to say 'all of them' but then the IT support people have to have a sample of every device available. Suppose, for example, your core corporate communications app works very well indeed through a browser on the desktop. So you allow everyone to use their own device BUT it looks terrible on the small screen allocated to keyboard-bearing BlackBerrys. And it defaults to 'mobile view' on iPads even when the screens are big enough to take a full desktop version. Are you sure you want to try to support everything?

App development: you will need to ensure your apps work on future versions of devices as well. This is, of course, very difficult – one company gave up and allowed its users only to use two models of BlackBerry, saying if they wanted to use something else, fine, if it worked – but if there was a problem the IT department wouldn't fix it.

Screen resolution: one major software vendor fell foul when Apple released the higher-resolution 'lenticular' versions of its displays on iPads. It simply didn't work.

Security: so, you're encouraging your users to use their own phones or laptops – but what about the integrity of the data on them? How do you secure it and lock it down? One answer is to go exclusively through the cloud, but that can be problematic when there is a connectivity issue.

Lost or stolen device: employees will need to agree what happens when they lose a device. One answer is to have an off switch that will zap everything on it completely. If you register with Apple, your iPhone or iPad can be set to do this from the Apple website. Remember, though, that there have been instances in the US in which people have reported their personal BYOD phones missing, the employer has wiped the phone and then the owner has found it, only to realize their personal pictures and music have been wiped too. Contractually, this is reasonable enough; to the employee who's just seen their photo archive of their newborn baby demolished, it's less good.

A word of caution: it's perfectly right to choose your own device(s) and select your own apps but be careful in choosing your own communication toolset. You may end up in a confused digital Tower of Babel. Check what communities you will be working with most and line up with their UCC or social networking tool, or make sure the variety of them have a digital Esperanto equivalent.

So, what's coming next?

No self-respecting author tries to look into the future with any certainty. Author Guy once edited a book called *Top Companies of the Future* and hopes fervently that most copies have been pulped; some businesses have thrived but by no means all.

So what's likely to come next? A few years ago, there were demonstrations of 3D video conferencing which looked promising as long as it could be achieved without glasses. However, in both the US and the UK experiments with 3D TV have been toned down or abandoned. The 3D revolution may not be as close as it seemed.

What's certain is that people will want sharper and sharper images as they continue to build their video presence. Standard definition may work OK but once it's possible, because of better compression and bandwidth, to achieve high definition – and ultra high definition (a new standard of about four times the resolution of a high definition TV) – conferencing, it's going to be difficult to turn back.

The more natural a conference (audio or video) feels the better it's going to be. And this is where some of the larger installations from people such as Polycom or Cisco score very well indeed. They use entire rooms and have mirrors reflecting an image rather than a camera pointing over the top of a screen, so participants can look straight into each other's eyes rather than talk to someone's forehead. This will improve communications. Or will it? An incoming generation is perfectly accustomed to using Skype on a laptop and not worrying about whether the eye lines are right. They don't use email; like IBM's Suarez, they prefer the more collaborative and archivable social media. Audio quality will continue to improve; the sort of conversation someone can have over an earpiece now was science fiction a decade or so ago.

The other major incoming factor has to be wearable technology. As the first edition of this book was being written, Samsung had become the first major brand to offer a smartwatch, mostly as a controller for a tablet or smartphone. Google Glass, meanwhile, has demonstrated how information can be overlaid on a pair of spectacles (whether or not this is a good idea remains up for debate). Contextual intelligence is also going to be important; think of it as a much bigger extension of companies such as Amazon offering you books it thinks you'll like, being able to assess much more about what's going to be appropriate and helpful to you in your life.

In terms of wishlists, the authors would want to add something about proper intercommunication: the non-confused Tower of Babel, as mentioned earlier. Different IMs being able to talk to each other and a business being able to acquire another without having to deploy an entire IT department to make the systems integrate without a struggle would be good. There are, of course, too many vested interests at work to make this happen too quickly. Curiously, Sir Tim Berners-Lee decided to hand the World Wide Web over to the public domain because he didn't want a British Telecom-owned web that wouldn't talk to a Microsoft-owned Web and so forth; this was a wise move, and it's precisely what's happened with the privately owned enterprise communications platforms.

But what's really on the horizon? Well, in the early years of the new millennium, nobody would have predicted the iPhone making smartphones so popular. We mention this because it illustrates the true perils of trying to future-gaze too much. Predict that Apple would be selling entertainment products and turning computing into a pocket item after so many others had failed with organizers? No, we wouldn't have predicted that. And it changed the shape of the consumer electronics industry forever.

What's coming next? Other than 'faster, more accurate and we'd like better eye lines please', we haven't got a clue.

Action points
for professionals

Look at your personal technology and your home internet connection. Is it good enough or do you need to talk to your employer about a major upgrade?

Consider your phone skills and how you communicate. Are you among those who have let your spoken skills lapse? And how can you upskill yourself as wideband voice becomes more important?

If your office has a BYOD policy, look at your device in terms of screen size and its technology – are you asking your tech support people for too much?

Action points
for managers

Evaluate the technology you are using at the moment.
Do you have the tools to communicate in front of you?
And does the employee need to be in the office to
use them?

Consider your technical infrastructure. Will it stand up to
a vastly increased amount of video traffic? Is the video
image you can get engaging enough for your employees
or colleagues, or should you be looking to upgrade as
soon as possible?

Culturally, how much of your communication is actually
allocated to the right channel? Consider using email as a
secondary tool; look into the social alternatives. And
revitalize voice communications in HD.

Measure this against all sensible business metrics. Is it
delivering against business criteria?

Chapter Three:

Teaming While Apart

WORKING IN HYBRID TEAMS

REMEMBER-FLEXIBLE, SMART WORKING ISN'T JUST FOR SENIOR MANAGEMENT

In this chapter we will discuss:

- The new way of work – how to work like a freelancer, in which the employer and employee work together for a mutual aim.

- Mastering collaboration – letting go of command and control and working towards mutual benefit.

- Acoustic intelligence and how it can be achieved – and why the human ear is not something you should muck about with.

Smarter working culture

Let's skip back to the 1970s for a moment. None of this flexible or smarter working stuff had even begun; workers and management were a considerable distance apart. The government, certainly in the UK, was often held in thrall by the unions. Effectively the unions representing the workers would tell the government what it could and couldn't do. This was, of course, a ludicrous state of affairs and not for any party political reasons. Party funding came into it by all means but fundamentally, both worker and government – or management – would have had the same end-game in mind: a better business or public service organization, making profits or surpluses for its owners, treating the people at the rock face reasonably.

The change that had to happen was simple. All sides had to learn to trust each other.

OK, the 1970s was a peculiar time by most standards and some of the feeling was based on historical antagonisms between management and working classes that should have been consigned to history decades previously.

But is it so different in your organization? Let's take an example from Andy Lake, Managing Director and Editor of *Flexibility*. The problem he had with a lot of smarter working implementations was that they were handled as a reaction to a specific issue rather than something applied universally. In other words, the scenario is that a worker comes to a manager and makes a case for whether they can do something flexible. The reaction is likely to take account of the personal circumstances of the worker as well as the business.

You have to ask: is this such a step forward? Really? Forelock-tugging worker comes to beg a favour from management – that's a favour likely to make him or her more productive?

It is far, far better to have an element of trust built in throughout the organization's DNA. The need is to jettison the traditional employee-employer relationship in which the employer buys the staff's time and effort for money and convert it into a productive working community based on positive contribution and mutual benefit. The other thing that needs to be achieved – and which is far from easy – is to put this into practice in such a way that it does not end up looking like a piece of linguistic window dressing.

Feelings can start to run high. Annie Leeson, author of several of the reports quoted in this book so far, was working on corporate strategy for an employer who insisted his employees should be present rather than work remotely. 'It was utterly demoralising - I was working ridiculously hard to try and win new business as well as delivering projects and, I thought, the least you could do is to trust me. If I take a break it's because I really need a break, because the rest of the time I'm putting in such a huge amount of energy.'

This is a fairly typical example of the right business result being delivered and trust still not happening. Leeson ended up going freelance. 'I realised that by working for myself, I have more control over my own productivity. I can put in a huge amount of energy when I'm ready to and not when my brain isn't in the right frame of mind.'

The culture of a modern workplace needs to exist on the basis of trust, and this isn't something that can be given in half measures – it is either there or it is not. Leeson's own paper, *The Topology of Work: a Catalyst for Change* (published by Plantronics in 2009) says as much and sets out a framework in which this trust becomes embedded rather than an option – and the changing nature of the workplace is very much a part of this change. 'People can no longer guarantee to be co-located, in the same space, for a set time period, every working day,' she writes. The rewards, as we've outlined in the introduction to this book, are considerable; the challenge is also substantial.

One of the areas in which Leeson's work is particularly strong is the move towards a new work dynamic. Managers have to be aware that empowering employees is not a simple matter of dressing their relationship up in a new way but of rearranging their relationship. Leeson highlights the following:

Culture based on trust from day one, as stated above.

Employee and employer need to be on the same side. As already stated, the old-fashioned 'us and them' attitude has no place in a modern working environment and arguably never did. Both sides want a profitable business with sustainable employment; there are, therefore, no 'sides'.

Self-motivation: this should stem from the previous point. Freedom of choice will allow people to dictate their own working patterns and smarter working will follow automatically.

Collaboration will follow naturally.

Above all, if applied equally and consistently, this trust will end with measurement by results rather than presence.

Note, though, that nobody is saying everybody should be a mobile worker or be at home all of the time. As Microsoft's Dave Coplin says, this is a serious mistake; instructing people not to come in to the office for a day is as restrictive as telling them they should work at their desks 9 to 5. This is about working wherever and whenever it is most appropriate, using personal as well as professional criteria to assess this.

Trust

It is a capital error to assume trust is somehow a soft, intangible benefit.

In his book, *The Speed of Trust*, Stephen M.R. Covey suggests trust has the potential to 'create unparalleled success and prosperity in every dimension of life' but says it's completely underestimated as a possibility. More importantly, he dismisses the idea that it's intangible, stressing rather that it's a solid and beneficial thing that can be grown and worked upon.

He outlines a number of solid strategies to help build it, as well as demonstrating its actual financial value (he has no time for the notion that it's intangible). It is not exclusively character-based, he says; it depends on competence as well. One could add that this in turn depends on context; ask the two authors of this book to be competent in pulling a publication together and we can do it, therefore establishing trust; ask us to perform brain surgery or pilot a passenger aircraft and we can assure you, there are more trustworthy candidates!

Covey divides trust into five waves, breaking it down usefully:

Self-trust

Before anyone else will trust you in business, you need to trust yourself. In smarter working terms this involves believing that you will perform tasks to deadline and with the desired outcome without direct supervision – if your colleagues are to take this seriously, it needs to be real to you.

Relationship trust

Individuals with whom you interact will learn to trust you as you establish self-trust in your life. Covey identifies specific behaviours that engender this sort of trust; the book is well worth reading for depth on these, which include integrity and other factors such as congruence and intent.

Organizational trust

This is how leaders establish trust in their organizations, regardless of which organizations we're talking about. There are people who trust their colleagues but work for an organization they mistrust, which is counterproductive when it comes to smarter working. An organization that offers it and provides the equipment but, crucially, whose employees believe this is simply a way to get further work out of them unpaid, is unlikely to find the new way of working is a success. The essential means of overcoming this is to communicate extensively with employees, make sure leaders are aligned with corporate aims and keep talking so that there is buy-in throughout the organization.

Market trust

None of the above is any use if nobody outside the business trusts the organization. Clients need to trust it, of course, but more importantly in the flexible/smarter working world the potential employee needs to trust it as well. It's all about reputation and every business leader understands its importance. Quality offerings and word of mouth in the marketplace are the best ways to get it out there.

Societal trust

This is trust in which – easy to write but less easy to achieve from a cold start – a company contributes to society somehow. Society begins to trust in the organization and over time it inspires other people to contribute in the same way.

For the flexible working environment the first four are the most important – employees need to look forward to working with an organization and embrace any new flexibility for what it is rather than question its merits/bias in favour of the employer.

Transitioning your organization

Leeson is also very strong on how to facilitate any transition:

Start at the top. During our interview, she confirmed that there are examples of working practices changing from the roots up, but strong leadership is a much easier way for effective change to happen.

Communication: after leadership has championed the change to smarter working the people have to understand why this is happening and they need to want it. Change must happen from the inside.

Pace and coordination: a multi-discipline team needs to work on this from the inside. Consider how education will keep up with any physical changes and also who needs to be involved – Plantronics' combination of bricks, bytes and behaviours (in other words facilities management (FM), IT and HR) made an excellent three-pronged attack on changing things.

Remember, as Leeson says, it affects everyone. Even the jobs that can't be done remotely – an absentee receptionist would be difficult to imagine, for example – needs to understand how and why the organization has changed, who this benefits and how.

Norma Pearce, head of Europe/Africa HR at Plantronics in the UK, finds some of the argument around human dynamics can be hard to quantify with the decision-makers. 'Productivity has certainly increased [since we adopted smarter working] but whereas it's easy to talk to the decision-makers about sales, this can be more difficult. I know people who'd go to the ends of the earth for this company. We have lowered absenteeism and increased attendance and headcount, certainly.'

So, how is this sort of 'discretionary engagement' (in HR terms) achieved? The answer for Plantronics was 'start early', which has something to do with the company's retention rate of 95.5% (this being the percentage of people who intend to stay with the company for the foreseeable future).

Plantronics' journey to smarter working

Pearce is the first to cite the business' holistic 'bricks, bytes and behaviours' model as one of the reasons for this success in retaining people. In terms of exactly how to implement a policy like this, she is equally clear. It needs the following:

A steering committee headed by someone senior:
Ideally, this committee should involve facilities management, information technology and HR personnel – each of these parts of a business needs to change if flexible working is to succeed. Pearce points out that many of the people visiting Plantronics in the UK to see how its smart working functions have not actually involved their HR departments sufficiently.

Measurement: workplace evaluation such as the Leesman Index can be a painful process to go through – basically, like holding up a mirror that has been somehow calibrated to search in particular for warts and down points.

Surveys: the staff must be encouraged to buy into the idea that this is their corporate revamp, nobody else's, early on. Their say in how the company shapes up will have a large impact on how any changes pan out. This has to be seen as a major part of the business' growth; Plantronics achieved 80% participation from its staff, at least partly because senior management had made it clear that this was where they had their say in how the business would change – so they either put up or shut up, right now. The analytical tools used were able to break down people's responses on the basis of age, gender, geography and department – and found concrete evidence against the idea that people would simply vote for 'less technology' if they were older.

Trust: not only the workers being trusted to perform their tasks remotely as discussed elsewhere in this chapter, not simply colleagues trusting each other to be working when they are off-site but also trust in the management. When senior managers had a request connected with flexible working and said they were working on it, staff had to believe they were indeed doing something about it and not fobbing them off with platitudes.

Autonomy: allowing the workers to dictate at least some of the pace of change. A good example is Plantronics' own move to softphones as distinct from landline phones; the company simply left the phones in place and slowly the vast majority of the colleagues asked for them to be taken away as they were not using them.

How smarter workers team up

The end result of all of these changes is a new human dynamic between associates or employees and their managers. If you are a manager, you will now need to consider how this affects:

The way you manage other people: they will no longer require close supervision as they will share your aim, to make a thriving business that works for both of you. Their lifestyle will have improved as a result of the changes to the workplace so there will be no need for the big-stick approach.

Remote working: people who are no longer located on site will – or should – be working towards defined management ends that work for both sides.

Connecting as a team: the way this happens will have changed, possibly beyond recognition. People will learn to interact better with absentee colleagues and trust each other to continue fulfilling corporate objectives.

The workspace part of the new working culture will change dramatically as well because there will be fewer fixed points of working. It is an exaggeration, and one people see often, to suggest there will be none; someone who is, say, a professional speaker or a pro footballer will do better on the whole if they turn up to the venue of the event at which they are expected. People's relationship with their space will change. If the task at hand comes first they will start to look at their physical placement in different ways, which is why having the right acoustic sensibility and zoning will help make a workplace right for multiple tasks. Above all, as we outlined in the previous chapter, it needs to be underpinned with highly robust ICT. Rock solid and reliable, underpinned by service level agreements and a clear understanding of what happens if it goes wrong.

A lot of this book has been occupied by the physical make-up of the workplace, whether this is the topology of the office or the appropriacy of the remote office. However, as Leeson points out in her first report, the people need to change to work in whichever environment they find themselves. It is therefore essential to adjust the human dynamics as well as the physical ones – and this is where the HR department comes into its own.

Finally, there need to be support structures and services. People working from home or in places outside the usual workplaces may be prone to feelings of isolation or they may miss the buzz of working in a friendly place. This is something that can be managed, avoided and helped, and good management means you'll ensure it doesn't become an issue. Information that might have been on the noticeboard before needs to be on the intranet and people need to come into the office from time to time so that they feel like part of the team. In British Telecom's smarter working experiment, people were asked to come back into the office after a year. That was arguably the exact point at which it was discovered that 'home-working' shouldn't mean working exclusively away from colleagues.

Managing with a looser grip

There is, of course, no guarantee that any other business will react and behave in the same way that Plantronics did faced with this sort of change. Why should it? Nonetheless, it may be worth noting that the biggest challenge the company faced when putting its smarter working policy into place wasn't the foot soldiers or the more senior (in age) members of staff; it was the line managers.

This may be useful to note if your own smarter working implementation starts to go wrong – the logjam may well not be the people who have to work with the change but with those whose task it is to implement it.

Kevan Hall, in *Speed Lead*, takes into account all of the changed relationships and helps managers by outlining how people are likely to respond in this changed work dynamic. He refers to having a 'finger on the pulse, not a grip on the jugular', which makes a lot of sense to us.

You first need to accept that employers and employees are probably more skilled and sophisticated now than at any point previously in history. This results in delay and cost as analysis paralysis takes its toll. The current management model for many people in complex organizations is still to control things centrally, when in fact very few people can comprehend a major corporation centrally. So how come they are expected to control it that way?

It is more sensible, suggests Hall, to take advantage of the modern preference for autonomy and allow people to work together in that way. A useful comparison he draws is with a ship; the captain doesn't have to know exactly how the engines work (although he or she will be a better commander for having some sort of insight into that area) – the job is to keep an eye on the waterline. This is where the water will be if the ship is running normally. If there is a hole above it then it needs fixing, but it's not an emergency; if there's a hole below it then it's a crisis.

Translating this into business, the manager needs to ensure that all of his metrics are above this imaginary waterline and be aware of issues that might drag the business down – such as inexperienced or poorly trained staff, or malfunctioning technology – but not to be so proscriptive that everything has to be micromanaged. Move control of the individual processes closer to where the action is happening, he recommends, for better outcomes. This, in turn, means building on local capability and slowly trying to replace a lot of the rules with responsibilities. So, 'You will sit at that desk and make eight sales calls an hour' becomes 'We need two sales a day, decide for yourself (or your team) how you can best achieve them and bring me the results'.

Staff and management end up happier and more productive as they all feel they have taken part in building the company culture. They are associated for a common purpose and cause.

A new corporate disease – meetingitis

Wiktionary defines meetingitis as 'an excessive propensity to hold unnecessary meetings' and the Urban Dictionary says it is 'having so many meetings that you cannot get your work done'. Either definition holds true of a very modern and damaging phenomenon in office life today. Too many unfocused meetings literally drain the energy, focus and motivation from a workforce. Nobody enters the workplace armed with the skills to effectively host meetings or be an active participant in meetings and they tend just to learn from the (mostly bad) habits of the company they work for. Dispersed working creates an added challenge of virtual meetings (aka conference calls or video conferencing) with audio challenges and participants checking emails or browsing the internet. Is it any wonder that meetings have become unproductive? Managing with a looser grip, also means arming your workforce or yourself with the skills to be more productive. A few tips to help make meetings effective and energized:

1. Circulate the agenda with the meeting request.

2. Any materials that will be reviewed in the meeting

should be sent 24 hours in advance, allowing everyone to get up to speed before the meeting and not spend time reading in the meeting.

3.   If the meeting is virtual, ask all participants to be on mute unless talking, while sharing a screen when talking through slides can help make a meeting more engaging.

4.   Set the scene at the beginning of the meeting – why we are here, what we aim to achieve – and set the time limit.

5.   Sum up at the end of the meeting: agreeing action points, timings, etc.

6.   Follow up the meeting quickly with an email that everybody can reference.

When to collaborate (and not)

Collaboration has become another one of those industry buzzwords the IT community is so good at pushing out. Clearly people have been collaborating throughout history, and in many different ways. Technology enables us to get rid of a lot of inessential and inefficient 'collaborations' – and it's created a fair few of them along the way, as anyone who works anywhere will attest.

Kevan Hall's *Speed Lead* is a definitive work on what might be described as 'unravelling the pasta' and what a waste of time so many meetings are. He examines in particular the definition of what a team actually is – including interdependencies and an inability to get a task done without the other members. Roles may overlap but essentially the people have different skills to contribute and they need each other, communicating regularly and depending on each other's services. Groups are different – they may work together, they may not, but they are grouped together. They work on objectives needing 'individual work and concentration', he says, and the individual roles don't overlap.

The inevitable question is: where do you and your organization sit on the collaboration spectrum? Are you a team at all, and if not do you need to invest in complex collaboration technologies and change management practices? Once you've established where you are in this, you can start to make productive decisions. The best teams are small, he suggests, so keep them that way and they will function better; it's also instructive to check meeting agendas and other interactions to find out when groups – which don't work together as frequently – are trying to address team issues and vice versa. Misunderstanding the sort of collaboration you actually need is going to be counterproductive all round – loosely federated groups won't be able to address the micro-issues that a genuine team can solve efficiently.

Insights into the sort of group or team you're running at any time will be instrumental in deciding memberships and permissions for collaborative technologies and which messages and interactions people need to access.

The potential power of solitude

Could being alone without distraction actually be productive? As a manager in today's always on, always connected world, should we encourage solitude among our staff as a way of developing deeper thinking and creative idea generation? Yale scholar William Deresiewicz thinks so; he challenged the plebe class of the United States Military Academy at West Point to consider the central truth that we must learn to think, to consider life deeply, in order to discover the abundant courage to lead and live with conviction. He believes that we don't have thinkers anymore. People who can think for themselves ... who can formulate a new direction for the country, for a corporation or a college ... a new way of doing things, a new way of looking at things. People, in other words, with vision.

He sees solitude, including reading instead of tweeting, as essential to the authentic introspection that means talking to oneself, the focused work that lets us trust ourselves, to begin to ask the questions we aren't supposed to ask, to learn to trust your own counsel when the hard decisions count, when all you have is yourself. Worth considering as a modern manager, with 24/7 access to information and a speedy work pace; developing people to really think things through (rather than consulting Google) is sure to be a huge strength to any organization!

New skills for virtual collaboration

Collaborating with colleagues who are habitually not in the same room requires a different skill set from the predominantly face-to-face form of working together. We say 'predominantly' because the dispersed worker will be in the office from time to time, and the office-based team may have to catch up. There are differences in the ways people will work together when they don't see each other all the time, though. Annie Leeson's report, *Home Working – Lost in Translation*, has a lot to offer on the subject. She identifies the virtual nature of interactions with home-workers and suggests the level of change this involves in the work dynamic is underestimated – the loss of face-to-face contact eliminates body language and facial expression and some kinds of interaction are hit harder than others; home-workers, however, are rarely taught the skills they need to compensate, she argues.

Speech impact

Beyond providing good equipment and networks, the professional needs to be trained for maximum impact in their communications. This entails all aspect of the presentation practice:

- Messaging and storytelling

- The art of producing good visual material

- The choreography of on-stage performance

- The mastering of speech

On the latter, Crawford Communications created the Speech Impact Course for Virtual Collaboration. It:

- Explains how the human voice works and why it is best to stand up while talking for maximum impact, even if remote

- Teaches the four Ps of effective virtual voice communications

    Power– if you think you're talking too loud, you're just loud enough

Pitch – the variety of tonality will keep your audience interested

Pace – talking at good pace will invite your audience to 'pedal with you', whereas slower talk will dramatize/emphasize

Pause – important to solicit reactions or questions

- Reminds of the power of storytelling/examples and not just reading of slides

- Educates on all things speakers and microphones (where are they in your smartphone?) and how to make best use of them

Andrew Leigh's book *Charisma* explains that seven out of 21 characteristics of charismatic leaders are related to effective command and use of voice and speech. So, if you invest in speech impact training it might propel your career as well.

Acoustic ergonomics

Ergonomics as a field has evolved dramatically over the years. Organizations such as the Federation of European Ergonomics Societies and tco.org (more on this organization later in this chapter) in Sweden have set the scene for ergonomics, environmentally friendly and ethical information and communications technology and are now respected authorities on how to treat a workforce.

One of the most crucial elements of this ergonomic debate today is the acoustic side. Let's face it, one of the most used muscles in information work is undeniably your vocal cords. So why is it, then, that the use of our voice and the support for it is so neglected?

Many organizations pride themselves on their awareness of their employees and their needs. Emotional intelligence is valued in business: the ability to sense how a meeting is going or how it isn't, effectively taking the temperature in a room.

It is surprising, then, that so few companies are aware of the strain they can put on people with poor audio implementations. We already covered the scenario: you have a meeting in the coffee area, which is cordoned off by beautiful-looking, shiny glass barriers, the polished wooden floor echoes the design – it's a gorgeous thing to look at and most people will be proud to work there. Unfortunately if you're over 45, it's documented as fact that the human ear deteriorates as the body ages and that too much noise reduces voice intelligibility and hence concentration. This is an entirely respectable thing to happen, it's not an illness and, of course, the experience gained by the colleagues of a certain age more than compensates for a little physical weakening here and there.

Sound business

Julian Treasure is the author of *Sound Business*: he suggests that there isn't much to choose between home and office settings when it comes to managing the level of noise – frankly, there's just noise.

He identifies four steps to getting good sound: acoustic design, noise control, an appropriate sound system and content design. 'Acoustics are the base,' he says. 'I'm just finishing an audit now of a shopping mall where there's a reverberation rate of three seconds where people are eating, and it's unbearable.' A reverb rate – the time it takes sound to dissipate – of about one second is advisable, he says. 'If you go over a second you tend to end up with a thing called the Lombard Effect, where the noise tends to escalate – it's the thing that ends up with us having to bellow at someone when we're a foot away in the restaurant.'

The key is to ask whether the noise in the space hampers progress. The aim of the acoustics stage is to eliminate things that amplify this noise. Avoiding rooms with parallel hard surfaces (generally called 'walls') can be difficult, but furniture and bookshelves can be added to dampen the noise down (books actually absorb quite a lot of noise). You can also buy sound-absorbing panels with things printed on them online.

This is important because of the effect it will have on the professional worker. Office workers, for example, may not realize why they are more tired than expected by the end of the day but tired they will be. Noise has major consequences, as Treasure explains. 'It's often been noticed that when the police come in to look at scenes of violence or even murder, they have to turn off loads of things – radios, TVs, music players. Noise tends to create stress.' It's not just a case of noise being bad for productivity, though; a teenager may think they are better and more productive while listening to loud music on their headphones. They won't be if you compare them working in silence to them working with distraction – BUT they may refuse to work without the music, or take longer because of an almighty sulk.

Many noises in a household will be curable, he says. An electric light buzzing, for example – the sort of thing you don't notice until you consciously listen. 'You have to ask, are these things actually helping me?' says Treasure. 'Sometimes they might – they could be masking another noise, for example.'

Sound systems are also important if you don't want to work in complete silence. Working on an aeroplane or train with sound-excluding earphones works well; other people like some sort of support sound and need to address what sort of noise will help. For the majority of readers of this book, we suspect, something unintrusive and undemanding is going to be the best help; personal taste is obviously very individual but something that will distract attention is highly unlikely to help a knowledge worker. Remember, this is highly situational and personal; a driver might respond best to something livelier to relieve the monotony, for example.

Other than that, most of the audible 'rules' are very much the ones that apply to the office – with the caveat that you're unlikely to be designing your home from the ground up. One final thought: if you're in a social situation and prefer to work with a little music, or want to transcribe an audio and there are other people around, use headphones. To do otherwise, Treasure explains, is what's known in the trade as 'sodcasting'…

However, thoughtless design can compound the problem. The coffee bar mentioned above will reflect sounds and echo around as if it had been designed specifically to obscure the detail of someone's speech. Add the clatter of shoes on the wooden floor and the sound being bounced around the glass partitions and you have a recipe for almost certain difficulties among the not-actually-all-that-old workers. Some foresight and sound insulation and the issue could have been completely overcome.

Acoustic intelligence

Acoustic intelligence, in essence, is the progressive realization that our voices are crucial in our professional and private lives. It's rooted in a profound understanding of how humans speak and hear and how audio instruments such as headsets and speakerphones can make the difference in effective capture and reproduction of human voice when co-workers are dispersed.

The foundation is audio ergonomics, where the audio endpoints are perfectly designed to suit the professional and protect him from unwanted and dangerous sounds. The Achilles heel is voice intelligibility: as voice travels through headsets, handsets, networks, software, all elements must preserve and pass on undistorted voice as produced on the side of origination in high fidelity. This is easier said than done.

The analogue telephone networks were built on baseband voice (up to 3 kHz) and are insufficient to provide full psycho-acoustics. The new voice-over-data networks can offer wideband voice (up to 7 kHz) but require all elements in the chain to do so. That's currently the exception rather than the rule. Good audio instruments will also eliminate unwanted noise and deal with network artefacts as good as they can. You will for sure have experienced that the audio quality of voice calls has deteriorated down the decades as mobile phone networks and voice-over-data have introduced intelligibility issues.

Even if the right audio instrument is used and good voice intelligibility is provided by the network chain, then the impact of speech is only as good as the quality of the speech that the speaker is offering up, which is where diction and voice articulation training comes in (see earlier on speech impact).

VOICE
= CRITICAL FOR DISPERSED WORKING

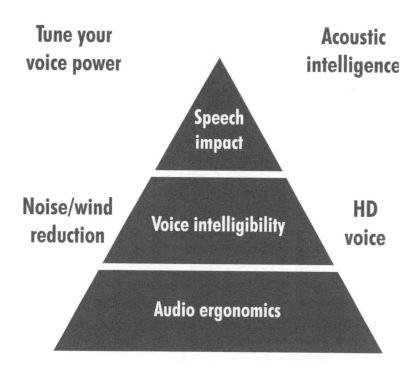

Tune your voice power

Acoustic intelligence

Speech impact

Noise/wind reduction

Voice intelligibility

HD voice

Audio ergonomics

Acoustic Intelligence, Simply Smarter Communications, Plantronics

Ergonomics

The other area that remote workers need to examine very carefully indeed is the ergonomic side. Treasure has outlined the audio components that are so important in a sensible workplace, but there are many more.

This isn't the point at which we advise you about getting an ergonomic chair and not sitting at the kitchen table to do all of your work. These elements are important but you've heard them a thousand times before.

No, this is the bit where we remind people that self-monitoring is important, not just in a work and task-driven sense but also in a looking-after-yourself sense. When working remotely or flexibly it's easy to overlook just how much is done for you by a good employer. It's not for nothing that Annie Leeson identifies obesity as one possible outcome from extensive flexible working. Here are a few things to consider:

Eye strain: is your monitor too bright, too dark, in a poorly lit room? Where is it in relation to the window or other sources of light? Ideally your desk lamp should point down at your keyboard so you don't get glare from it but you do get enough light to read by.

Breaks from the screen: medics recommend a break every 45 minutes or so. It's appallingly easy to overlook this while you're at work in an office – peer pressure means you won't be inclined to take those important breaks. Headaches can ensue.

Too much sitting? Leeson's point about obesity is well made. The daily commute is a major inconvenience and – to use the scientific term – a faff for people on a daily basis. Eliminate it and initially the sense of wellbeing can be considerable as the journey to work morphs from a battle in the rush hour to a wander into the spare room and taking a seat immediately.

Only this doesn't actually do you any good because you haven't left the house. Calories that would have been burned up by the simple act of moving about a bit now hang around – repeating this frequently means it builds up over time. Lethargy, increased risk of diabetes and heart disease, high blood pressure as fat builds up and increases the risk of stroke... we don't want to alarm you or anything, but good health isn't something the remote or smart worker can take for granted.

There are many strategies. Take control of your environment as far as you can (this is going to be tricky in shared spaces but you can pick and choose where you work). Get up and move about a bit. Some people who work from home extensively have had success simply by buying a dog – they take it for a walk in the morning and that's their walk to work; they take it for a walk in the evening and that's their walk back home!

TCO Development

TCO Development has been advancing sustainable IT internationally since 1992. Its mission is to ensure that ergonomic, environmental, social and economic considerations are included in the manufacture, use and recycling of IT products. TCO makes it easier to include sustainability criteria in IT purchasing, and verify those criteria are supported by TCO Certified certification. The company is owned by TCO, a non-profit organization based in Stockholm, Sweden.

20 years of advancing responsible IT

TCO Development is widely recognized for TCO Certified, the international sustainability certification for IT products. Certification began in 1992.

Milestones to date:

1992 – the first TCO certification is introduced, focusing on low emissions and reduced energy consumption in displays

1995 – criteria to reduce hazardous material content: chemicals, flame retardants and heavy metals

1999 – ISO 14001 required, tighter criteria for display image quality and visual ergonomics

2000-2009 – stricter environmental criteria in line with technology developments buyer demands

2007 – Headset Certification criteria for performance, usability, emissions and much more ...

2009 – requirements for social responsibility in production introduced

2012 –launch of new generation TCO Certified, the sustainability label for IT products

Health and safety in focus

The background to TCO Certified began in the 1980s as computers were gradually introduced into office workspaces. As people began to work more with computers, health and safety concerns emerged. Poor ergonomic design and high levels of electromagnetic emissions were cause for concern, along with high energy consumption. At that time, TCO began working with users and industry to develop mutually beneficial solutions.

Action points
for professionals

Don't fall into the same trap as many offices have done, decorating for looks rather than function. You can buy professional equipment for your home and the basics, such as a proper desk and chair, are essential.

Set up your space, get the right height on the chair, desk and screen (which should be eye height), and invest in a proper keyboard and mouse.

Movement will help increase your energy, walk about a bit – keep yourself sharp and keep the quality of life high. You may achieve more with shorter hours solidly at the computer.

Examine your virtual communication skills and don't rely on body language too much – you will not have it in a virtual setting.

Keep your hearing in trim – don't abuse your ears with loud music. Look, we don't want to depress anyone but it's going to start fading as you get older anyway – don't hasten it!

Action points
for managers

Establish a common aim between management and ground-level workers – this is a matter of communication and leadership, and is essential if any real collaboration is to work.

Orient your management style around the tasks and the people that perform them – the building comes last and should serve the first two.

Assess your management style – are you micro-managing or could you pass responsibilities on to others?

Listen to your office when it's empty. Literally, hear what the background noises are, and whether they are conducive to getting the work done.

Look at how you can implement zoning for the four Cs – concentration, collaboration, contemplation and communication. They all have different requirements.

Chapter Four:

The Smarter Professional

BECOMING A VIP

In this chapter we will:

- Explore the broader context of work in your life.
- Clarify the new freelance work style.
- Ensure you understand your capabilities and personality.
- Introduce the basics of career planning.
- Make sure you fully understand what productive dispersed working entails.

Work/life balance is a lie

Many people talk a great deal about their work/life balance and so do many managerial books on the subject. People have to fit in their work and their family, they need to look after themselves so they have to keep fit, take time to relax, indulge in interests they may not share with their families, as well. They need to be performing at their best and most productive when they are engaged in work tasks. So they need to ascertain some element of work/life balance. There is a whole industry surrounding this concept; motivational speakers talk about work/life balance, HR departments look at work/life balance and sometimes pay expensive consultants to come in and speak about it.

There is one word to describe all of this. Phooey. Unless you want the authors to come and speak to you at great expense, of course…

No, really, it's a nonsense. Google it if you like although we're not sure what you'd search for; you are alive when you are working. Therefore the idea of work/life balance is a ridiculous notion. Nobody talks about an eating/life balance, or a reading/life balance, or a balance expressed in terms of any other activity. This whole concept is something that should be alien to us; it's not your life and your work that need to be in balance but all elements of your life. This book is all about work but if you're obsessing about sport, a hobby, anything that's throwing your life out of kilter, it's worth looking at.

Working smarter is all about taking a task and performing it wherever it is most appropriately performed. Arguably, living smarter is all about the same thing – you're not rigidly 'at home' when you're spending time with your family, for example. So the balance between the two has to be flexible as well.

You need to establish in your own mind a number of things:

Where does work fit into your own life? There have been studies and entertaining quizzes in the media about what constitutes a workaholic; questions such as 'do you prefer staying in the office to going home and seeing your partner' abound. To us, that's more a question of whether your partnership is working or not – but that's a debate for elsewhere. The question of where work should be in relation to your own life is, of course, going to vary according to individuals and their circumstances. If you're an employee simply working for the money, that's one thing. If you're the entrepreneur building a business from nothing to pass it to your family, that's going to be different – and there will be many gradations in between.

What sort of work do you want to do to support your ideal lifestyle? At minimum, work should be a means to support you and your family – without that, it's not worth doing. It can also mean realizing your full potential as a professional. There's no implied judgment about people wanting to work simply as a means to support family, but in this book we're concerned with the second category – people who are really after life satisfaction rather than just working for a living.

Professor Peter Warr and Guy Clapperton said as much in their book, *The Joy of Work?* (Psychology Press, 2010), pointing out that it will mean different things to the same person at different stages of their lives. Early in the book, Clapperton points to an early role as an administrator of a charity that had better money and more kudos, including a title, than his next job as a junior reporter on a technology trade magazine; the latter involved a lot more going to the bar with colleagues after hours and for this and other reasons it fitted his 'balance' better. Later in life, he and other people no longer lived alone, they had families. They wanted to see their families so the previous amount of socializing would be seen as actively damaging to work/life balance. This is all about context.

So, one of the things you need to do is to give yourself an honest assessment of where you are in your life journey as well as your career. OK, we've got this far without mentioning the word 'journey', but it's relevant. Consider whether you're:

- Early in your career – eager to please and make new friends, maybe in a new town or country as well.

- Mid-career – do you want to own a part or all of what you do, or is there some other stake that's meaningful to you?

- Married, single, happy with that – do you have kids to consider, how important is family time?

- Late-middle of your career – thinking of some sort of independence, perhaps setting up on your own, perhaps becoming more senior in your existing workplace?

- Heading towards retirement and looking at legacy.

Happiness at work is important and, as Dave Coplin points out in his 2013 book, *Business Reimagined*, a survey in the US suggested that 71% of Americans were not satisfied with their job. This may or may not be duplicated internationally. If it is, then we need to reimagine our worlds of work.

Work 2.0

Coplin's is a classic example of a life that appears to be in balance. When speaking on the subject in public he's passionate about a number of things. One of these is that flexible working, of which he is a staunch advocate, is not a simple matter of getting everybody to work at home on Friday. Some companies have actually done this and it's no more flexible, he believes, than instructing everybody to be in the office from 9 to 5 on weekdays.

'Where we're at right now is that work is an activity, it's not a destination,' he says. 'It's something you do, not a place you go. And if you have that mindset then it transforms your understanding and expectation of what work/life balance actually means.' For him, taking control of his environment gives him complete control of his life. He freely acknowledges that a lot of this is because he's not on a production line or doing a job that requires physical presence. He's clear on a number of things that work/life balance is not. 'It's not a 50/50 thing between working and not working, it's infinitely variable. I can be working for an hour in the morning, then spending time with my family [while] probably checking on emails and keeping on top of things, then really dedicating specific times to specific activities,' he says. Writing his book, for example, didn't happen in the office but primarily in libraries because the place was right for the task. 'I knew I wouldn't be distracted. Or in the dead of night when the family was asleep.'

This is an area in which flexibility is paramount; working in the dead of night means getting up late the following day, but if that is how someone can be most productive then that is how they need to be managed. 'That's how I interpret the idea of work/life balance, it's giving me the employee the power to choose the best time and the best place for me to do my work, rather than arbitrarily come into a specific location every day at a given time.'

Results and meritocracy

Key to understanding how this works is an appreciation of how Microsoft, Coplin's employer, has embraced measurement by outcomes. One phrase used earlier in the book to describe the attitude the employee needs is 'freelance attitude', but from the employer's point of view this is a freelance attitude accompanied by the staff member's wish for job security, tax and national insurance taken care of, holiday pay and so forth.

Microsoft is on its journey towards full flexible working, says Coplin. He had worked for the company for eight years at the time of writing and said it had been consistent in its approach. 'I'm measured completely by outcomes,' he says. 'I'm not measured by process, I'm not measured by how many emails I send. I'm measured by customer satisfaction, projects completed on time.' Microsoft does not get involved in how he actually does his job. It gives him and his colleagues the tools, outlines objectives and then doesn't talk to him. 'If I want to bunk off tomorrow, or decide that the best place to work is the library, that's up to me.'

So far, so common to an awful lot of organizations. The next step is to make the flexible culture less reactive. Andy Lake, of Flexibility.co.uk, criticizes a lot of companies' flexibility as being based on exceptions and to an extent Coplin concurs. 'What tends to happen is that someone approaches HR, says they have childcare issues and need to work flexibly, HR puts a load of stuff in place and it happens' he says. 'On one level that's brilliant but on another level it's problematic. I've now got this special, unique arrangement with my company that none of the rest of the team have.' In Coplin's example they can ask for it but it's not theirs by default.

This may contribute to something Coplin and his colleagues have noted in their research into flexible working. There are trust issues, as might be expected when there is a new way of managing people around, but the problem is not trust between managers and employees. 'Trust is crucial to get right and what we found was that the issue was between employees. I work with a bunch of marketers, I'm out meeting and greeting and standing on stage and they wonder where I am. "Where's Dave" becomes a euphemism for "he's sitting on his patio drinking tea" and what we found from our research was that this starts to drive a very different set of behaviours.'

These include people trying to overcompensate for not being in the office while they work flexibly. This may not always take the form of productive activity; they will send more emails and make more phone calls to overcome the prejudice of others, but this doesn't mean they're actually necessary calls or helpful emails (see the previous chapter and Luis Suarez's view of email).

To eliminate this, Microsoft will now be working towards making flexibility a strategic imperative. This is not a bid to make employees happy, fine though this is as an aim; rather it is an acknowledgment that engaging employees in this way will ensure that everybody wins.

Caveat: remote working and isolation

All of the self-determination outlined by Coplin and others should add to an overall sense of wellbeing. Cognitive neroscientist Dr Lynda Shaw, however, says the old trust issue is still relevant. 'In the commercial world I see a contradiction going on. An awful lot of managers perceive that if people are working from home they're not working, so they're very controlling and old-fashioned.' Her research tells her this is a complete misconception; people who work from home will typically be working harder than their office-based colleagues. 'They don't switch off. That machine, whatever they're working on, their laptop, their tablet, is on from the minute they get up to when they go to bed.' This can lead to isolation and depression, she says; she's seen it a lot and it includes senior people too.

A well-equipped and prepared company will be aware of this possibility and needs strategies in place to ensure people feel involved and part of something. The consequences, whether someone is physically isolated or in a family or co-working space but still isolated by tying themselves to their laptop or tablet computer, can be serious.

Arguably, this is the point at which flexible working ceases to be a solution to an individual problem and starts to become endemic within an organization. Coplin's and Microsoft's research shows that only 20% of people working flexibly are doing so for childcare reasons despite the popular preconception that this is why people want it.

It is, of course, up to employers to change to bring self-motivation and self-management to the fore if flexible working is going to deliver real benefits. 'This is about leadership rather than management,' says Coplin. By 'management' he means old-style management, which needs to see people the whole time and which doesn't understand that someone can be working when they are not being directly supervised. 'Flexible working doesn't do well in that environment where someone is saying: "how are you getting on today, what have you done, show me a status report".'

He breaks it down further. A manager, he suggests, will be given an objective by their boss, break it down into tasks and assign them to members of the team. A leader will ascertain the desired outcome, present it to the team and allow them to work out their own methods and timings. 'That's when the change happens. It's really about how you can get your management into that level of confidence, so you're not directing people but giving them the ability to make the right choices.' He calls this the anti-jobsworth mindset.

Obviously there are other processes that need to sit behind this mindset, to ensure people do the right things, their outputs and outcomes are measured and they are recognized.

Watch for exclusions and binary decisions

An important facet of this sort of working policy is that people must not end up excluded from the social and business elements of performing their tasks alongside other people. During research for this book and other projects, the authors have come across:

People finding out about an office outing of which they were unaware because they were not on site.

In the same way, people hearing about a five-a-side football match in which they would have liked to take part but hearing too late.

People generally feeling excluded from the office culture because they were working flexibly.

In many ways, this can stem from the old-fashioned view that 'working flexibly' mostly means working from home. 'It's not binary,' comments Coplin. 'Working flexibly means working where it's appropriate and that doesn't exclude the office.' It may not always be the optimal place to work but it's still important. Coplin certainly finds that if he isn't in the office once a week then it starts to get problematic. 'I start to drift out of sight from my colleagues, I'm not as connected as I could be, but it doesn't need to be more than once a week.'

This will be different for different people – once a week suits Coplin, twice a week or once a fortnight may be better for other people. Much of this is about what sort of communication works best for a particular employee or manager in a particular situation; there's face to face, then video, then voice and finally electronic communication.

Self-discovery and finding that great job

In the end it's all about finding out who you are and finding a job/role that's a great match for you. In the last chapter, we touched on adapting your workspaces and finding out, for example, whether you work best in a quiet environment or somewhere with a little more buzz or background noise, and how to adapt a home office setting to make this work better.

So who are you exactly and how does your special combination of competencies, skills and personality make you ideal for a role or assignment?

It is worth taking a two-centred approach before embarking on any career change based on the desire for genuine flexible working. Common sense dictates that every individual will be different and every job will accommodate different levels of self-determination. This is before different management styles emerge as a factor, and these will also make a considerable difference. So it's necessary to work out what is achievable and desirable for yourself first, and then look at the workplace and the business case.

Warr and Clapperton (op. cit) suggest that every job has a mix of 'needed nine features' to be fulfilling. Establishing where your personal preferences (or those of your employees) are in the mix will help understand what can be done to enhance your business using this information. The same authors also list a set of 12 'vitamins' – components of a job that need to be in balance in order to make it fulfilling. We will look at both here.

The most relevant of the needed nine features are:

Personal influence

Clearly, only someone who relishes personal influence will work well in a situation that demands a great deal of it. Associated with this should be an honest appraisal of how much of a self-motivator you can be (check Coplin's comments on education: recent school or college leavers may find themselves accustomed to a lot more direction than someone who has been in the workplace for a while).

Using your abilities

This may even involve using abilities not directly associated with your function. Microsoft's Dave Coplin is, in fact, attached to the Bing search engine; the impetus to champion flexible working inside and outside the company came from him rather than the company itself. As long as his core work is completed there is no problem – if you have an appetite for activities over and above your required tasks, flexible working will help.

Variety

A related point to the above – many jobs have a lot of variety built in, and many people will find a variety of physical spaces (including a well-equipped and set-up office) a boost.

Social contacts

Ensuring that you and/or colleagues will not be isolated if a flexible plan is put in place is vital. There are people who will be ill-equipped psychologically to be apart from colleagues for a given length of time (which will vary) and there will equally be people who find it impossible. Certainly when British Telecom set up its first working from home experiments early this century it found there were people who just wanted to get back to the office – it felt wrong for them to be away. Are you of that mindset? And how set is it?

Also among the needed nine are clear demands and goals, which is a general point about good management, money, a clear career outlook and a valued role.

Warr and Clapperton continue with an analogy of 'vitamins' needed to make people happy at work, adding three more features. Once again, the list is not exhaustively about flexible working but the more relevant elements are:

Supportive supervision – this is not something that can be sacrificed simply because someone is not in the office; however, ascertaining what balance of supervision you need as distinct from how much self-motivation you can achieve is essential.

Security and prospects – which may relate back to any prejudices felt by colleagues who are not convinced that flexible working does in fact equate to working. Anyone who is going to influence your career prospects has to buy into this if you are not to suffer personal disadvantage.

What type are you?

No matter what you're good at and what job you would prefer, your personality matters a great deal. How often does it happen that you've fallen in love with a job, started with loads of energy and passion, to find out a couple of months later that it doesn't fit you? Many then learn that their personality is at odds with crucial others. After some blaming of others and ultimate soul searching, they realize they never discovered themselves and how to work best with others.

Look at Bijoy Goswami's work such as *The Human Fabric*, in which he celebrates and investigates people's differences. He illustrates this by being different enough to include his music and poetry in the audio version of the book.

There are a number of speakers and writers, many of whom are quite persuasive, who will say we are all divided into different 'types'. Some of these are pretty useful; leadership coach Nigel Risner says in his book, *The Impact Code*, that people are all lions (straightforward and tenacious), monkeys

195

(dynamic, creative, energetic, attention span of a hamster), elephants (capable, analytical) or dolphins (very empathetic). This can be seductive thinking and as a very general guideline it has its uses; however, it's really, really generalized. You can be a different thing depending on the mood you're in and the task you're performing. We would counsel people, as gently as possible, to avoid being too glib about their type – and always to remember that if it sounds too easy to be useful and true, it probably is.

Goswami, however, has reduced things further to types that appear to work in a real-life context. He divides people into three categories based on the initials MRE – maven, relater, evangelist:

> **Maven:** this is the person who proscribes what will happen in an organization and sets the rules. Mavens are the innovators and they are essential, the downside being that they may not want to collaborate every time.

> **Relater:** the relater does what the name says – this is the empathetic person, the one who builds bridges and communicates. They may not innovate much but they are the facilitators of innovation. Think of the much-maligned Doctor Watson in *The Hound of the Baskervilles*: 'It may be that you are not yourself luminous, but you are a conductor of light', Holmes

says, ensuring not only that we understand the importance of the relater's role but we also see how deeply patronizing the extreme maven can be.

Evangelist: the one who does the selling of the resulting products – selling in the metaphorical as well as the literal sense, the one who broadcasts rather than goes for the one-to-one conversation.

Goswami is clear that nobody is 100 per cent maven, relater or evangelist, but every organization he has encountered works pretty much along the lines of needing all three.

Understanding your personality and that of those you work with is essential in establishing how you or your employees fit into this new world of work. Ask yourself:

- Does the job fit into flexible working?

- Does an individual fit smarter working?

- Do their colleagues fit working in this way – will they accept that their absentee colleagues are still working?

It's also worth considering whether 'employer' is the right word in the 21st century. Never overlook the possibility of a portfolio career, or freelance/staff blend. If smarter working has any overriding theme then it's surely to adopt a freelance attitude, paid for outputs rather than for methods; as long as it's handled ethically there should be no problem with this.

THE LAYERS OF PERSONALITY

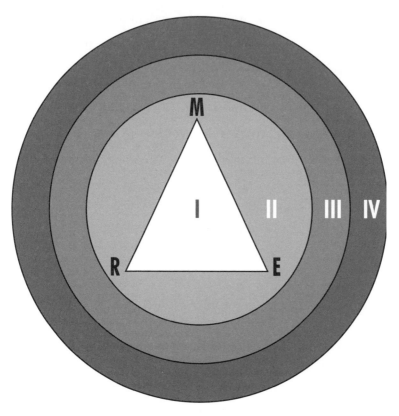

I Drivers   M Maven
II Values   R Relater
III Communications style   E Evangelist
IV Relationships

Source: *The Human Fabric*, Bijoy Goswami

Your next great job

Richard N. Bolles in *What Color Is Your Parachute?* offers not only insights but a systematic approach. The book itself is a guide for job hunters but its exhortation to establish your personal style is applicable to smarter working. He refers to getting a 'fresh inventory' of what you offer the world and what you are looking for, to come up with a new picture of a job that would excite and stimulate you.

He has a number of practical aids to help put this self-profile together. One is to make a graphic about yourself and prioritize all of the facets of yourself that you can think of. He also advocates describing yourself in seven dimensions:

- What you know

- What sort of people you like working with

- What you can do

- Favourite working conditions

- Preferred salary and responsibility

- Preferred location

- Goals or sense of mission and purpose

There are worksheets in the book to help you establish just who you are. This isn't as nebulous as it might sound. The person who interacts well with large groups or who presents well is not going to be the same as the micro-manager or number-cruncher and so forth.

Appreciating work from home challenges

So now you've discovered the very you and are in that great job. And it pays to be fully conscious of your personal living environment before you dive into dispersed working. There are assessments to be performed on your personal circumstances and living space. Flexible working is not, we stress again, all about working from home but about working appropriately for the task; however, in reality a lot will depend on your house's suitability as a working space. Questions to ask yourself will include:

- Do I have a good work space at home?

- If not, is there a good alternative convenient to me?

- Regardless of space, is home a suitable environment? Are there distractions (small children are a good example but there will be others).

It's worth looking at just how you use your home and whether this suits your lifestyle and requirements. Annie Leeson, in the aforementioned *Lost in Translation* report, identifies several scenarios in which the home is used as a workplace (see also illustration):

A – Overflow: in which work is taken home when it hasn't been finished or when there are exceptional events in someone's private life.

B – Alternative to the office: when someone regularly works from home in a structured way but the office is still the hub.

C – Home as hub: in which the majority of work is intentionally done from someone's home.

D – Home as a docking station: in which the classic road warrior keeps all of their equipment and information at home and then works there only occasionally.

E – Home as a live/work space: in which home is the only place work is carried out.

On many occasions these elements of flexible or dispersed work will have come about by accident when a flexible working initiative has grown of its own accord. It can be well worth checking with an employer whether there is scope for change on occasions when you're dissatisfied or think a more deliberate, planned approach would be better.

Leeson's *Lost in Translation* study gives an excellent overview of key pressure points related to working from home. The summary below categorizes these by whole lifestyle, life-scape and remaining integral to the organization.

HOME WORKING SCENARIOS

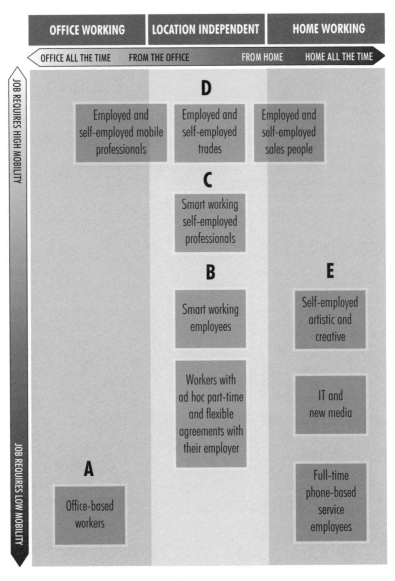

OFFICE WORKING	LOCATION INDEPENDENT	HOME WORKING

OFFICE ALL THE TIME   FROM THE OFFICE   FROM HOME   HOME ALL THE TIME

JOB REQUIRES HIGH MOBILITY

JOB REQUIRES LOW MOBILITY

D

Employed and self-employed mobile professionals

Employed and self-employed trades

Employed and self-employed sales people

C

Smart working self-employed professionals

B

Smart working employees

E

Self-employed artistic and creative

Workers with ad hoc part-time and flexible agreements with their employer

IT and new media

A

Office-based workers

Full-time phone-based service employees

A Home as an overflow
B Home as an alternitive
C Home as the hub
D Home as a docking station
E Home as live-work space

Source: *Home Working: Lost in Translation*, Annie Leeson

203

MANAGING A WHOLE LIFESTYLE

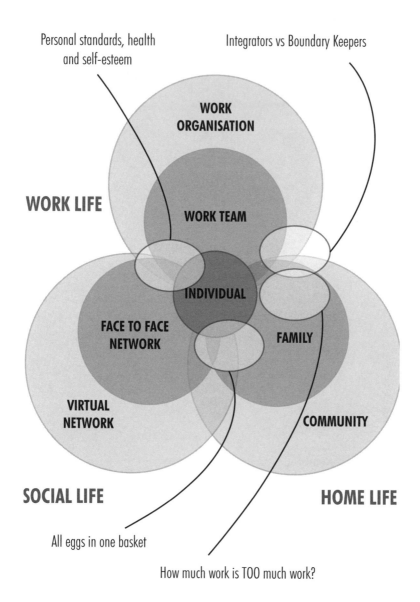

MANAGING A WHOLE LIFESTYLE – KEY PRESSURE POINTS

Home-working brings many benefits and is idealized by many people. However to achieve these benefits, the home-worker must manage a whole lifestyle not just a job.

Ensuring that work life, home life and social life are kept in balance can be challenging – key pressure points often arise.

Integrators vs boundary keepers

Home-working gives people far more freedom to choose how they work best. People tend to fall into two distinct behaviour patterns: integrators, who like to mingle work and home life activities, or boundary keepers who will strive to maintain a clear distinction between the two.

How much work is TOO much work?

One of the biggest issues for home workers (both integrators and boundary keepers) is a struggle between either working too much and not looking after themselves, or struggling with motivation and not doing enough work. However, overworking is the more common problem with home-workers.

Personal standards, health and self-esteem

There is still a prejudice in some countries (notably the UK, less in Denmark and Germany) that home-working is somehow an 'easy option'. This can gradually erode people's self-esteem, and even impact on how well they look after themselves and take care over rest, diet and exercise during the day.

All our eggs in one basket

If we live and work at home, issues in one area have a much greater effect on the other – we can't go to work to escape a problem at home and vice versa. Any disruption that occurs in the environment also has an impact on both home and work life as everything is happening under one roof.

MANAGING A LIFE-SCAPE

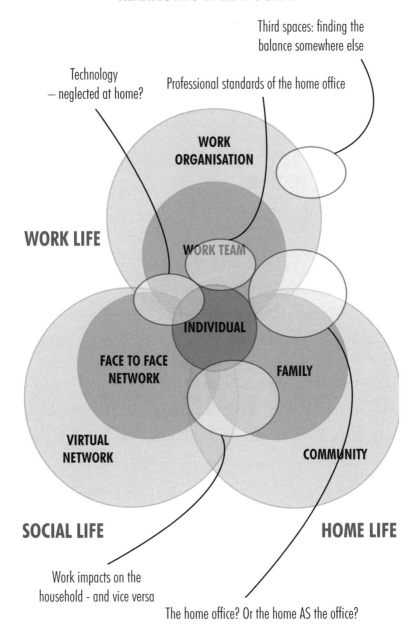

Third spaces: finding the balance somewhere else

Technology — neglected at home?

Professional standards of the home office

WORK ORGANISATION

WORK LIFE

WORK TEAM

INDIVIDUAL

FACE TO FACE NETWORK

FAMILY

VIRTUAL NETWORK

COMMUNITY

SOCIAL LIFE

HOME LIFE

Work impacts on the household - and vice versa

The home office? Or the home AS the office?

MANAGING A LIFE-SCAPE – KEY PRESSURE POINTS

Home-workers have gone from being provided a specialized, office workstation to having to manage their own 'life-scape'.

For ad hoc home-workers, the sofa or the bedroom make a welcome change from an office desk.

But for more frequent home-workers, creating an effective life-scape presents unique challenges:

The home office? Or the home as the office?

Do you have a dedicated room to work in? Or does your work permeate all areas of the home? Research has shown that as well as the use of time, integrators and boundary keepers can use physical space to delineate, or integrate, work from home life.

Companies find it hard to provide guidance on how to create and use the home as an office, because of the variation in available space and individual preferences. Even e-work, the virtual working training company, says their 'creating a home office' training module is often removed by clients who feel they can't interfere at home.

While this does allow for personal choice it can leave the individual worker with a staggering array of choices and little professional guidance as to how to put it all together.

Technology – essential but neglected at home?

Without the technology developments allowing people to connect to their work, home-working would never be practical on a large scale. The next stage is for technology to help people connect better with other people, not just to their work.

Because of the variety of personal preference, companies are often giving home-workers a budget, allowing them to choose appropriate home technology equipment themselves. This trend is creating a rise in the 'prosumer' – professional equipment being purchased by consumers rather than organizations.

However, as well as technology evangelists, there are also large numbers of home workers – especially among self-employed or small business owners, who are not investing in technology that would make significant improvements to the way they work.

Professional standards of the home office

Home-workers have the responsibility of defining and managing their own professionalism and professional standards. Even though they may be working at home, the image they portray to the outside should not necessarily reflect this.

Work impacts on the household and vice versa

When home-working is regular or full-time, the impact on the other members of the household needs to be taken into account. Conversely, being surrounded by your own domestic responsibilities can be a huge distraction for home-workers. Both need to be discussed and resolved through agreement with other household members.

Finding the balance somewhere else

Very few home-workers actually do all their work from the home office. Many people find that they can work best when they use a variety of different spaces for different types of work, and find their balance using a third working space. New types of third spaces, aimed specifically at home-workers, are springing up around Europe. These include work hubs, live/work spaces and co-working spaces. Employers are even paying for home-workers to be members, for easy access to well-equipped working space near to their homes.

REMAINING INTEGRAL TO THE ORGANISATION

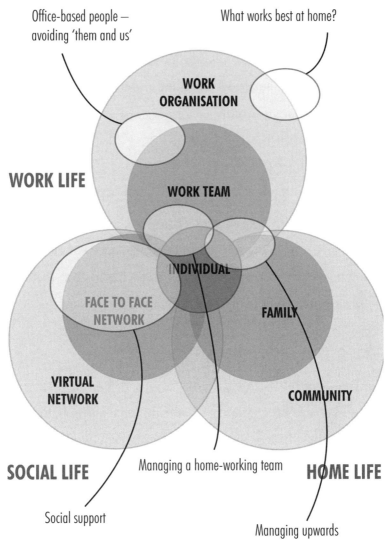

Office-based people — avoiding 'them and us'

What works best at home?

WORK ORGANISATION

WORK LIFE

WORK TEAM

INDIVIDUAL

FACE TO FACE NETWORK

FAMILY

VIRTUAL NETWORK

COMMUNITY

SOCIAL LIFE

Managing a home-working team

HOME LIFE

Social support

Managing upwards

Source: *The Topology of Work,* Annie Leeson

211

REMAINING INTEGRAL TO THE ORGANIZATION – KEY PRESSURE POINTS

From the previous sections, it's clear that home-workers have a significant shift to make in order to manage a new lifestyle that blends work and home more closely.

However in addition to this, the home-worker also now has the challenge of ensuring that they remain woven into the fabric of their organization.

Managing upwards

Maintaining a good relationship with your boss, and other leaders within the organization, is a key challenge for home-workers. Fear of being left out of the loop, and particularly of being passed over for promotion, means learning to manage these upward relationships is an important new skill.

Managing a home-working team

As a manager, keeping 'control' over a dispersed team can seem like a huge challenge – and this fear is probably the single greatest barrier to the adoption of home-working in an organization. But this is no surprise – a whole new management style and culture can't just be left to individuals to figure out, and won't happen overnight!

However, once it's business as usual there are huge advantages to managing a remote team. Basically, you cannot micro-manage home-workers. And established home-workers have relatively high confidence and independence in their work. As a result, their managers have more time to focus on the bigger picture.

Social support

'Social' aspects of being 'at work' are very important factors in making employees happy and positively affecting well being and motivation. As the proportion of time spent at home increases, how can employers ensure their home-workers aren't becoming isolated from the social support of work friends and colleagues?

Although home-workers spend less time in the company of work colleagues, it is critical that they still feel that they belong to a work-social community. Companies that don't actively promote employees coming together for social interaction run the risk of lower engagement, loyalty and resilience among home-based workers.

However, one advantage of home-working is that people have greater social interaction with their local community and people outside the organization. This can stimulate new ideas, keep people 'connected' to the outside world and develop a broader level of 'social skill' from interacting with a wider variety of people.

Avoiding 'them and us'

Another significant issue that home-working can cause is a rift with those left behind in the office. This can range from the mild inconvenience of having to coordinate with home-workers, to strong resentment and lack of trust. However, this is easily prevented by building mutual understanding, equality and transparency into the system.

What works best at home?

It's important not to assume that ANY or ALL work carried out in the office can be transplanted successfully into a home-working situation. For regular home-workers, coordinating the right work for the right location creates another layer of complexity they need to learn to manage.

In particular, in previous research we noticed a marked difference between the choices made by senior staff and the work chosen by more junior and less confident members of the organization.

Family life

Microsoft's research suggests that only 20% of flexible workers ask for flexibility because of their family. This is just as well because one area in which flexible working can hit people unexpectedly hard is in their home life.

'You have this infinitely variable schedule,' says Coplin. 'So it's not as though I can say to my wife, every Tuesday at 6 pm I'll be home. I might be, I might not – I might have been at home all day on Tuesday or I might be back late, I just don't know.'

The really tricky part can occur when a worker is at home but not available to his or her family. The challenge is to get managers and employees alike thinking beyond flexible working as a euphemism for 'working from home', finds Coplin. 'There's stuff to do, there's my books there, there are a lot of distractions,' he says. Young children in particular won't understand that a parent is physically present but not able to play/comfort/feed.

Partners, too, may expect people to be available for housework, or conversation (which isn't unreasonable as workplaces have their water cooler moments too) – working in a library or somewhere not dissimilar can be a useful alternative.

THE **SMARTER WORKING** MANIFESTO

Leeson's report also highlights some of the technological aspects of working from home in addition to those to which we referred in the last chapter. She predicts – you might say 'hopes' – that technology will go from connecting people to the workplace to connecting people with people. A lot of professional equipment is being purchased by consumers in anticipation that it will help them connect better; however, she mentions many are cutting corners. This is unlikely to help – economic reality is economic reality and not everyone is going to have access to the biggest and the best, but if an enterprise is going to work well then it's going to have to have a proper connection to its employees, all the right fonts on the system, so that a PDF isn't screwed up when it's shared, and a professional face when it addresses the world.

Ready to be a VIP?

Beyond workspace, Annie Leeson believes communication skills especially need brushing up in order to become a stand-out Virtual Interactive Professional (VIP). Tuition is recommended.

Clarity: meanings must be communicated clearly so that the recipients understand the correct meaning. Misinterpretations are easy online and, as Leeson points out, they may be difficult to recognize when the originator of the misleading text can't see the puzzled reaction of the listeners. She urges clarity, scripting of calls and frequent checks of comprehension, plus of course a decent, clear phone line.

The authors of this book are broadly in line with her findings, although we'd argue that a scripted call is no substitute for a good piece of communication in which one person listens to the other. Listening is a skill that's falling away just as much as speaking clearly.

Power: in a virtual meeting, Leeson says finding the right pattern of words to establish authority is a difficult thing.

Emotion: connecting with people is not as easy virtually as face to face and people need to understand this. Attitudes, nuances, humour (often a minefield even face to face if it isn't shared) are not as immediately apparent without visual cues; remote workers will need to find their own ways of expressing them.

Identity: Leeson calls this 'judging a book without its cover' and we can't put it better than that! All of the assumptions one might have made about someone, all of the 'first impressions count' bits of our culture are finished off or at least modified when someone is not physically present.

Context: face-to-face meetings tend, in the UK at least, to start off with some sort of small talk. How was your journey, you look tired, can I get you a coffee – all of these things break down the barriers between us (and sometimes baffle people from other cultures, admittedly). These can be substituted by offering some sort of verbal context to where you are, allowing for some sort of external noise. In Leeson's experience, people who have no contextual clues tend to blame the person rather than anything external when something goes wrong in a business relationship. Make sure they understand something about the context; human instinct is to have some sort of insight and take account of outside forces.

Rapport: this is again difficult without being face to face – learn to build empathy through the way you talk and above all become an active listener. Vocal equivalents of nodding and eye-to-eye contact to make sure people understand you're in agreement or not will all help foster trust.

Engagement: let's be blunt about this: it's really challenging if people are listening to your voice only, you don't have PowerPoint (this may be a good thing if, like many, you overuse it and have extremely verbose slides) but you need to hold people's attention on a conference call. Draw pictures with your words, tell stories, vary your pace a little – if you have multimedia at your disposal don't use it at the expense of engaging with people (if you're obliged to use PowerPoint or any other slide system have a look at a good book on the subject – Lee Jackson's *PowerPoint Surgery* is excellent and focuses on getting rid of words in presentations as far as is humanly possible).

Dynamics: managing a team when you can hear rather than see them can be a daunting thing. If you're presenting across the internet make sure the structure is rigid and people know when there are breaks – the temptation to zone in and out because someone is tired, the cat has just wandered in, they fancy a coffee or something (and don't see why they need to tell the other participants) can be strong.

None of this should look too intimidating; it's relatively straightforward and can be achieved by most intelligent people. Just don't underestimate the task of keeping someone engaged when they're not there. Likewise, when you're engaging with other people be sensitive to how much they need to know and understand that you're being attentive. The end relationship should be as productive as a face to face.

Elsewhere working

Should you opt for a portfolio career, working between home and a fixed office, then it's important to organize a portfolio of working spaces as well. This is something often overlooked by managers who assume 'work from home' or 'work on the road' will take care of themselves.

As earlier described, there are three forms of workplace to juggle, in the authors' view. These are:

- Office

- Home

- The third space

This third space might be described as a mid-point between the two – a shared space where there is WiFi, a workstation but which is owned by someone other than the employer. There are coffee shops, of course, but there is also a new breed of shared workspaces springing up. Some are spartan and scruffy, some are hubs based in the heart of the City of London (and probably other cities) and wouldn't disgrace the most fastidious professional.

Richard Leyland developed a fascination with these and explored a number when he took on a lot of freelance work in 2007. He first had the idea to develop a database for roving workers; this slowly turned into an idea for an augmented reality app, called Worksnug. Receiving eventual backing from Plantronics, this has a social element and reviews shared working spaces worldwide.

'I realized there were good places in London to work and there were terrible places,' he says. 'I also realized it was terribly romantic, this idea of mobile work, with ideas of freedom, self-determination and flexibility; in reality it's extremely different, you can be let down by very practical factors like noise, expensive coffee, poor WiFi...' Reviewing the venues on the grounds of these practical elements became a passion. 'What I thought I'd do was get to the bottom of what was good in London and what wasn't, and share it.'

He notes that his typical user likes control and personalization and suggests improvements all the time. Something that is emerging but which hasn't taken off yet is this co-working space idea, but that's likely to emerge.

Flexible spaces internationally

There is a lot of commonality among the requirements for flexible 'third space' areas internationally. One of the leading providers is Regus Business Centres, which answered a few questions for us:

What's the demand for flexible workspace like internationally?

'There's growing international demand for flexible workspace. First, mobile technology means people can work anywhere. Second, globalization is sending businesses and individuals into new countries and continents, and they need a place to work.

'Third, you have rising entrepreneurship in Africa and Asia. People are using serviced and flexible workspace to set up and grow their businesses. Fourth, firms are reducing CRE (corporate real estate) expenditure through more flexible workplace strategies. In a KPMG study in 2012, 60% of companies had increased their use of virtual workspace over the previous three years.

'And finally, businesses are using flexible and remote working to attract and retain staff. In a global Regus study last year, 48% of senior business people said they now work away from their main office at least half the week.'

What sort of flexible workplaces are available internationally?

'As demand for flexible workplaces increases, we're seeing more people start to provide flexible workplaces – small local providers and so on. There's a big range in terms of the quality of workspace out there, so it's important for businesses to understand what they want from a flexible workspace – e.g. do they want 24-hour access? Is a prestigious address more important? Do they want access to meeting space or video-conferencing? Do they want a virtual office or physical workspace? And so on.'

What do users demand from flexible workspaces on offer?

'One can't generalise too much about this, because companies use flexible workspaces for so many reasons: to house temporary project teams; to explore a new market; to let staff work at more convenient locations; to save money compared to fixed office space; to outsource property management. But generally, flexibility, convenience, and value are at the top of requirements.'

'Users require different things in different markets. For example, in Africa, oil has brought a surge in demand for flexible workspace, and because of the infrastructure problems in many markets there, our customers depend on us to make sure that utilities such as electricity and telephone networks work reliably. And because finding experienced support staff can be hard in some markets, they value the quality of the staff in our business centres. In other markets, other criteria may be important – from offering a choice of locations, to being able to access ready-to-use international workspace in a city where that is scarce.'

'Multinational companies want access to a global network of flexible workspace. They want one go-to flexible workspace provider that can help them do business wherever they want to. It saves them negotiating terms with multiple local providers, finding local lawyers, visiting endless workspaces until they find the right one. This all slows down their expansion, as well as adding to admin and legal bills. So using global providers like us who offer a large network and consistent standards makes their growth easier and quicker to execute.'

'Location and convenience are crucial. In Beijing, for example, an important criterion for a recent client was having a location close to specific metro lines, so its staff could get to work easily. That was crucial to staff morale. The fact that we offer such a wide choice of locations in many cities is very important to our customers. As cities grow and traffic congestion worsens, a choice of convenient locations will become even more important.'

'Another important aspect for mobile workers and business travellers is security, consistency and reliability. If they use flexible workspaces in a new city, they want to know that they'll be safe, that their belongings will be safe. They don't want to go into an office and not know what they're going to find there.

'Consistent standards boost users' productivity, too. For Regus Businessworld customers who use our business lounges across the world even in a new centre, they can immediately log into the IT system, etc, and get down to work fast. They don't have to waste time trying to work out how to use the space.'

How do the different workspaces apply in each culture?

'There's a lot of local variation, so it's important to understand local preferences and approach each market individually. But also it's important to understand our customers' preferences and cultures.

'For example, many technology and social media customers want teaming space in their offices. But in some markets and countries, this may be a new idea, and existing workspaces may have to be adapted to provide that. So it's about meeting the culture of the customer as well as the locality – especially since we usually have a mix of local and international customers in our business centres.'

The practical factors Leyland notes are the mundane, ordinary things. Noise level is the most popular; expense and speed of WiFi and location of power points are also important but so is the intangible 'cool' factor. Is this a nice place to be?

This is why the co-working space is likely eventually to take off. 'There is no trend (yet) towards co-working, alas,' says

Leyland. 'I consider myself to be part of the global co-working community, I've been co-working for a very long time and have probably visited more co-working spaces around the world than anyone else on the planet.' The corporate world has yet to buy into the idea, he suggests. 'HR and facilities teams within businesses are conservative. The managers of the co-working spaces need to communicate effectively with those sorts of people and deliver the sorts of model they want. The people that define the kit that mobile workers have in companies, and the health and safety elements, that's a conservative lot – and while they know people work in coffee shops and train stations, they haven't yet engaged in helping them in that working style or nudging them towards it.'

The benefits will be many when it happens. The cost of a seat in an office, the length of time for which a seat is occupied in an office, all point to flexible working being the way forward – but the move towards encouraging people towards co-working as a model has been slow to arrive.

Mentoring and training

One area that's missed in many organizations is that individuals need training in order to work from home. It does not go without saying that someone will need to be:

- Motivated

- Able to work without distraction when away from their peer group

- Free from distractions including children, pets, spouses

- Able to hive off an entire room for their workplace (when their partner had the idea that they had a share in the entire house).

There are numerous approaches that can help overcome these practical difficulties, except probably the last one. Concerningly, nobody trains someone to work from home or to manage based on outputs rather than face time. As Coplin pointed out earlier, this starts as early as school when people are told where to go and when in order to work. It continues with a lack of mentors or role models in the freelance or home-working world. It can be worth considering buddy schemes, investigating shared premises where they are recommendable and continuing in that vein.

Start with education

Schools and to an extent universities tend not to prepare people for flexible working. It could be that we have to acknowledge the need for considerable change if flexibility is to become as endemic as it needs to be.

Microsoft's Dave Coplin points out that self-direction, a project portfolio approach managed by a motivated worker who can manage himself or herself, is not how students are taught to learn. 'Kids start at the bottom of this institution, they progress through a really structured, managed timetable that takes them through a cycle, every year they move up a step within this organization – university is a little bit different but mostly it's all managed for them. What I worry about is that if you come out of the education system and go into an organization that really understands how flexible working benefits them and wants to collaborate, you have no skills in that area. How do you self-manage? How do you handle the empowerment you're being offered? I think we've got to start being mindful about that and help people develop those skills.'

Are you suffering from partial attention disorder?

When you are on conference calls are you distracted by emails or texts, or browsing the internet? Are you in a face-to-face meeting but still feel the need to constantly check your messages? If you have to focus on completing a task, do you do it or are you tempted to check Facebook or any other social media platform? If you have answered yes to any of the above, you could be suffering from a very real condition called partial attention disorder.

Advances in technology have enabled us to be connected all the time, but this does not mean we need to be connected all the time. The fear of missing out has induced an addict-like behaviour where many are obsessively checking messages. This is counterproductive as it takes focus away from the task in hand. You can gain control again with a few simple measures:

- Turn email off if you have to focus on a task – it will get easier.

- Dedicate certain times during the working day to answering emails.

- Put your phone on silent and switch off vibrate during face-to-face meetings.

- Try to put sensible limits on social media use.

Action points
for professionals

Assess where your work/life balance actually is.

And also assess how you're getting on lining up a series of jobs/assignments that really tap and value your potential.

Perform a self-test to establish where you fit into flexible working.

Perform tests on colleagues to establish how well they fit and into which jobs – are their main strengths as mavens, relaters or evangelists? Beware of over-generalizations.

Establish in your own mind and those of your colleagues that 'flexible' can mean working in the office, working in a shared space, anything.

Assess your home realistically – in what way are you going to use it?

Action points
for managers

Ask what people actually do and why they need to function in a particular place. Centre around the task and the individual rather than the location.

Accept that there will be changes – and develop strategies to help colleagues who may no longer fit in to the niche they did previously.

Survey your employees for an honest assessment of whether they're going to accept remote colleagues.

Educate where necessary and establish that colleagues who are away can indeed work productively.

Chapter Five:

The Smarter Organization

ORCHESTRATING SMARTER WORK

In this chapter we will:

- Talk about concrete first steps in evaluating your state of flexible working and what needs to change.
- Examine how to approach your workforce to ensure changes happen.
- Bring together the three disciplines, bricks, bytes and behaviours, to make them work in tandem and deliver a smarter organization with a smarter workforce.

Orchestrating smarter work

So, you've started to put the changes in place and you think you've done it. The flexible working ethos is working, it's paying its way and you're happy. OK, think again. It's never over. You need to keep revisiting it if it's going to pay its way in future generations – they'll want different things from us, you've got to keep it fresh.

Readers of previous chapters (as distinct from people skipping to the end to see how we finished – you missed a great bit in chapter 2, section on UCC; that was a high point) should by now be aware that smarter working isn't a matter of a few tweaks. It's an undertaking involving real root and branch change in an organization. This will involve corporate culture as well as management style. We can't say it often enough: smarter working is a wholesale change journey affecting leaders, management, associates, absolutely everybody in an organization and elements of the building that houses it.

In this concluding chapter we hope to offer some further practical steps – the 'get your hands dirty and change things' section. Ultimately, smarter working has to be driven by the top, though. If you're reading this as an employee wanting to change an organization from the grassroots up then it can be done but only with a solid business case to impress the people who will make the decisions.

If you're a manager, then you need to be ready for the blocks in middle management as described in Chapter Three, and also to undertake the change on three practice areas – bricks, bytes and behaviours – in a true integrated multidisciplinary effort (see illustration on next page).

Also note that although for convenience we refer to this as 'the change', it is of course an ongoing process. The elements that will satisfy a workforce in 2014 will bear some relation to those of 2020 – things haven't changed as quickly as that – but there will be differences. An incoming generation will have new expectations we may not have anticipated yet.

What is unlikely to change is the need for engagement with the organization. This needs to happen through each of those three practice areas.

FOUNDATIONS OF A
SIMPLY SMARTER WORK IMPLEMENTATION

ALLOWING ASSOCIATES TO WORK WHERE AND WHEN THEY ARE MOST PRODUCTIVE, COST-EFFECTIVE AND ENVIRONMENTALLY RESPECTFUL

BRICKS

- Work topology
- Activity based working

BYTES

- Unified communication and collaboration

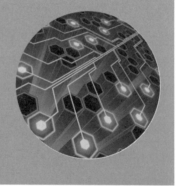

BEHAVIOUR

- Manager and associate virtual interaction skills

Source: *Simply Smarter Working*, Plantronics

Empathetic, involved leadership

This book has already referred to the need for Philip Vanhoutte or another 'big beast' (in the words of facilities manager George Coffin) at Plantronics to get the move to flexible working taken seriously, but it's a point worth making once again. Without that leadership, without someone senior championing the new ethos, it won't get adopted and it really is as simple as that. Leadership from the top is absolutely essential.

Louis Lhoest at Veldhoen is one of the authorities on changing approaches to working in this way. He starts from the point of view of 'activity-based working'. 'What it means is looking at how we support people to perform their jobs and their tasks in a particular way, especially looking at how organizations can support the activities people carry out in the best possible fashion,' he says. Note that he starts from the person and how to support them rather than telling people what to do. Many businesses start with the organization and its own structures and job titles, which is rarely effective. Instead, taking the business' needs, the values people want to carry in their lives and desired outcomes and ensuring that the organization supports people in fulfilling them in the best possible way is a much better practice. 'One of the conditions is the physical environment, the work environment itself; other conditions are the IT and collaboration tools and how you train people and, third, the behavioural guidelines you have as to how you do things.'

This is an important point to bring out. Smarter working centres around the individual to a very large extent but it cannot be a free-for-all. People have mentioned adopting a freelance attitude to work when they are working smarter and on the staff; this doesn't mean that the organization revolves entirely around them. It is all about freedom of choices within the team, and organizational perspective.

The centre of the analysis of how a business is performing, in Lhoest's view, therefore becomes the activity. This is fine in theory, but what are the practical steps? Lhoest's approach is generally:

- Survey his client based on what they do and where they work

- Establish what percentage of their time is taken up by each task

- Discuss what they need to perform these tasks optimally

An example that reflects the modern environment harks back to Luis Suarez's ethos on collaborating virtually. People collaborate on video as well as face to face and collaborate on documents; they may be collaborating for an hour, an hour and a half, so among Lhoest's recommendations would be some sort of provision for extra privacy. 'Traditional work environments don't offer that because it's either open space or an enclosed room, and there's very little between them.'

Naturally, a strong lead is crucial to make this work. It needs to be shot through the organization. There isn't one definitive form of leadership that will make this work, says Lhoest. The most important thing is the connection between the business drivers, company values and the operatives and how it translates into the working practice, he says: 'Make that connection and there's a very strong possibility that people will get engaged, because everybody wants to contribute in some way or another.' Simply connect why behaviours are required to change with the business changes that are being asked for and people will carry them out, every time. 'Managers need to walk the talk, they need to demonstrate they are doing what they are asking and leading by example – and aren't afraid to make mistakes.'

The result is an increase in profitability most of the time, managers will be reassured to hear. Reduced costs, increased productivity through better collaboration and more enthused employees are all among the benefits that should become apparent very quickly.

Does smarter working pay off?

The ROI question for smarter working will come up at various points in the journey. At Plantronics Europe and Africa the following benefits have been achieved since the full implementation of all Space, Technology and Human Resource change plans as introduced in 2010, as measured in a variety of surveys and analysis reports:

Fixed asset rationalisation

- UK office space reduction - from 47,440 sq ft to 21,154 sq ft

- Cost savings from real estate $400k+ per annum

Business operating efficiencies

- 40% cost savings on outbound calls

- 65% cost savings because of no internal call costs or conference call costs

- $120k+ cost savings from removal of deskphones/ reduced travel/standardized equipment

Workforce metric improvements

- Voluntary turnover reduced from 15% to 3.2%

- Attrition reduced from 12% to 2%

- Absenteeism reduced from 12.7% to 3.5%

- 40% improvement in employee workspace satisfaction (Leesman pre and post occupancy survey)

- Improved employee engagement – result in 86th percentile (industry norm is 69%)

- Improved retention – 'intent to stay': result in 98th percentile

Appreciating your organization's needs

The best place to start such a fundamental change programme is from where you are at the moment, as Lhoest says. This sounds obvious but not everybody does it – the idea of 'top down reorganization' can be taken to mean the top people having an idea and insisting it should be imposed on the ground-level staff.

This might just work if those at ground level agree with the top level view. As a scientific approach, however, it leaves a great deal to be desired. A well conducted scientific survey is the only way to ascertain what's really happening in a company.

One is the Leesman Survey, already referred to in this book. This is the brainchild of Annie Leeson and Tim Oldman and it contains a lot of searching questions on established workplaces. They have seen many changes in organizations as a result of their input.

Common faults in existing companies include:

Closed mindedness: organizations call themselves innovative or entrepreneurial but in the event turn out to be quite risk-averse. Leeson believes that 'risk-averse' and 'entrepreneurial/innovative' are the reverse of each other.

Poor collaboration: many organizations put the word 'collaboration' on the end of what they do but despite claiming this as a virtue, in harsh economic times they are in the habit of battening down hatches instead, remaining siloed despite their intentions.

Being blinkered about what happens in other industries. A publisher might look at what's happening to other large publishers, for example, but will typically be unwilling to look outside its immediate market. Likewise, bankers will see the entire world in the language of what other banks are doing; they need to get inspiration beyond their sector.

Measurement

The Leesman Index (at leesmanindex.com, unsurprisingly) is essentially a temperature check of where companies are and how happy their employees are at a given time. It is best conducted periodically – many clients opt for once a year – but there are a few caveats. If readers of this book at employee level wish to use it or commission the owners to ask some other questions with a view to making structural changes at work then it may not do the job. Leeson has the following reservations:

If employers are scared off by negative results, they may suppress rather than act upon them.

If employees perceive that this sort of survey is going to bring about rapid change in their interests, they could have their expectations managed artificially high.

If she were a workplace strategist wanting to implement smarter working, she would not lead with Leesman but find another way in, she suggests.

The index itself is a substantial questionnaire that should leave businesses with an excellent idea of where they actually are in terms of readiness for smarter working and other changes, with substantiation. Tim Oldman began his work in architecture, designing for the transport industry, then moved into exhibition spaces. Here, throughput was essential as was a feeling of permanence in a temporary structure. He had to report about circulation and how many people could get through an exhibition stand. He then moved into retail and designed premises where everything is measured, then went into office design where, beyond some measurement to do with health and safety, he was stunned to find that the performance measurement of the spaces he saw was woefully lacking. This seemed wrong to him, so he started to become intrigued with tools more traditionally associated with management consulting or employee engagement.

He then started working in corporate transformation but found himself back in testing fairly quickly with his work topology theory. 'I then had dinner with an ex-client and after years of lobbying her on the merits, she'd just done the Myers-Briggs psychological profile for work. We discussed the insights and learnings it offered her individually and I explained that was essentially what I'd been trying to do for businesses: a standardized workplace profiling technique – a health check in a standard form.'

It was then she who questioned why nobody had tried to do it before and they discussed how a global standard would develop a powerful insight into the value of corporate offices. Oldman dug further and was surprised to find nobody had already put such a thing together. He got back in touch with Leeson and the Leesman Index took shape. His aim was to address the workplace as a physical space and infrastructure, aiming at the facilities managers or their equivalents in organizations. Anyone wanting to use the Leesman Index will need to bear in mind that this is where it's targeted – the 'bricks' part of Plantronics' multi-disciplinary Smarter Working implementation methodology.

Changes people make

People are often surprised by the results of the questionnaire. Oldman compares it to going to the GP and being sent for an X-ray; the report will go into that sort of detail. 'We had one client in financial services that came out so badly in every area the client said it was a blood bath. All of the bars on the graph were red rather than green; he felt as though he'd had

247

a bloody nose. The design team that inherited the project were probably delighted, though, because it meant that whatever they did, it would be an improvement.'

What can be more interesting is when something comparatively cheap and simple can make a great deal of difference. A client had solid green bars on the chart except for two or three lines. Oldman takes up the story: 'It was a large company with four buildings and one of the areas in which the score was bad was internal signage. One of the buildings had a new influx of population but the buildings weren't labelled on the outside so they had to remember which building was which. So they put some graphics on the outside.' This year the survey was repeated and the bar had turned green; total cost perhaps hundreds rather than thousands of pounds. 'The survey goes beyond what architects will typically look at when they're designing the office,' says Oldman. In another instance, the room booking system had gone wrong; people were booking and not taking the rooms up, so people who had nowhere to meet would be surrounded by empty offices. A little internal housekeeping went a long way to repairing good feeling in the organization – the ergonomics, the technology were right but the block booking of rooms simply hadn't worked.

Leeson adds that this is very much the sort of tiny detail that makes a smart working initiative succeed or fail. 'You can see the small physical or protocol things that create problems and might be hindering people.'

In 2013, Leeson and Oldman had a look at overall trends and found that the most important things in a workplace were the people elements. Both at the top and the bottom were the 'social cohesion factors', as Oldman calls them, which were universally high in the top performing workspaces. Leeson identifies a few of the elements needed to make this side of the business work:

- Social interaction

- Meeting colleagues

- Accessibility

- Relaxation – tea/coffee facilities

This is where Oldman's theory of the 'topology of work' becomes important – things that are apparently sidelined in an organization through remote working strategies will inevitably end up surfacing elsewhere. 'It's like chasing a kitten under a duvet,' he says, adopting a metaphor originated by Leeson. 'You press it down and it'll come up again somewhere else. So if an executive team tries to compress something out of the workplace, it'll crop up somewhere else.' So if there's a social interest, for example, it will crop up elsewhere.

It may not be a cost saving – you might spend more once you've measured workers' needs

This is the point at which readers who want simply to save money through flexible working should probably look away. 'Far too many managers see flexible working as dispersing activities elsewhere, off their radar, but these activities are still needing to happen somewhere and if these activities have an impact on corporate organizational bottom line, should surely be considered and supported?' This isn't just about reducing spend, in other words, it's about investing as well.

It's not just the soft benefits that can involve spending more money. One of Oldman and Leeson's clients, a facilities management company, will need to budget for more maintenance because dispersed workforces start to treat the office like a hotel and expect it to be maintained for them rather than by them. One example is that if there are coffee cups left by a dishwasher the remote worker will leave them there while the office-based staff will be minded to put them away. Tiny things like that will add to routine costs. Additionally, people who use the office as part of a portfolio of workplaces will expect higher quality as they have the choice. If an office's chairs are uncomfortable then they will decamp back home or somewhere else, pronto!

Smarter working coaching and toolkit

There are a number of areas to identify in which management can change subtly. Leeson, certainly, is convinced that flexibility in the workforce necessitates not an overall change in management but better application of proven management styles. 'All of the research I've done shows that it's not different ways of managing people that's required, just "better quality" management. So all the organizations that decide not to bother are missing out on the opportunity to completely upgrade the leadership and management capabilities of their staff.'

The key skill to revise, she says, is coaching. 'Coaching is a manager supporting someone to do their best work, and that is different from telling people what to do,' she adds. 'If it's done well it results in people working well under their own motivations rather than being somewhere because they have to be in order to be paid.'

In a nutshell, there is a definite need for a smarter working policy. And in using survey tools such as the Leesman Index, physical and virtual infrastructure needs can be discovered. Do give good attention to acoustic zoning and solid, dependable ITC. From thereon, detailed smarter work design is all about the specifics of the job and the professional that is assigned to it. Most importantly: train and coach.

When looking at the job itself: can it be done remotely without a negative impact on the business, preferably with a positive one? Second, the person who is doing the job – will they be able to self-motivate and do they have the right premises at home, or will they need further coaching? Plantronics uses a checklist called LISA – Location Independency Suitability Analysis. Verify first for the suitability of the job or set of activities for remote or flexible working, then have a look at the person involved.

A good leader will then look at the space layouts desirable for work, as far as possible putting Myerson's four acoustic zoning Cs into practice. Concentration, contemplation, collaboration and communication need different areas. No, you can't control your employees' homes and nor should you; however, you may be able to question them on just where they will be working and why. Tim Oldman found in 2013 that the majority of home-workers were still operating in nondesignated areas such as kitchen tables and might be doing themselves some harm in the longer term; is this something you can afford to have in your business? Likewise, hotel bookers will need to be informed of the need to work on the road so somewhere without WiFi will no longer do.

Elsewhere we have written about the ICT demands of remote working. A good process will include the use of smartphones, headsets, car kits, tablets and all those pieces of equipment as appropriate, but it will also assume the IT department needs some say in which tablets exactly as any corporate applications will have to render correctly on the screen. The ICT infrastructure under the building (larger organizations will definitely need fibre) will need to be fit to the task.

Finally, training is the life blood of what might become a virtual enterprise. Managers reading this book might assume people will know what to do and have considerable initiative when it comes to self-motivating and self-training. They might. Equally, they might not. Training on the new tools is a given; training on how to work remotely, how to respond to the new sort of manager who suddenly no longer needs to see you, is very important as well. Plantronics used www.e-work.com to produce custom associate and manager training and added e-profiler, a software tool that allows associates to personalize the toolsets they need for the job.

From the manager's point of view rather than that of the employee, what remains is to measure business progress. Specialist tools will almost certainly be essential for this; Plantronics found those at www.successfactors.com were well focused on results rather than processes.

Homebound – how contact centres leverage homes

The phenomenon of employing home-workers to perform customer contact roles is truly an idea that has come of age. A growing body of evidence is emerging that home-working is on the verge of becoming both an acceptable and highly effective option for both private and public sector organizations.

Historically, home-working has been dismissed by some in the contact centre world (and in society more generally) as being more suited to creatives or the self-employed than to people serving customers of major brands, or for public sector organizations from councils to health authorities.

However, attitudes are shifting and today a Londoner paying a parking fine incurred in Westminster is likely to speak to a home-worker in Dingwall, hundreds of miles away, who will smoothly handle his enquiry from a Highland cottage. Technology is dismantling the barriers to doing things differently and there are signs that psychological barriers are being overcome too.

Where there was once general scepticism that the kind of work done by agents in traditional contact centres could be done outwith the confines of a tightly-controlled and centralised environment, we now detect a dawning sense of enlightenment that not only can things be done differently by using home-workers, sometimes they can be done better and at lower cost.

The type of people coming forward to take up opportunities in home-working are often of a higher calibre in terms of educational attainment than those who generally work for contact centres and it is breathing new life into an industry sorely in need of knowledge workers.

Yet there are still significant impediments that may hamper further growth in home-working in the UK and which must be addressed at the highest political level if the benefits of home-working are to accrue to more businesses and to more employees.

Paradoxically, people already running successful home-working operations report in the UK Customers Contacts Association (CCA) Members' Survey that reliability and speed of broadband connection is not a problem; yet for others, broadband remains a major concern.

The answer to the paradox may well lie in the fact that a high quality broadband connection is a prerequisite for effective home-working; therefore those running operations successfully will have selected recruitment locations with this in mind. How much faster might the home-working revolution spread if there were universal access to high speed broadband across the entire UK?

The UK is a digitally smart nation, with Britons ranking as the most active users of the internet in Europe's top five economies, yet the UK still lags behind Germany and Spain in superfast broadband coverage, with speeds of higher than 30 megabits per second only available to two-thirds of the population.

Investment in broadband has a vital role to play in helping the economy back on to a growth trajectory, generating sustainable social and economic growth, and boosting innovation. Yet a third of taxpayer-funded superfast broadband projects have yet to commence, which must surely threaten the feasibility of the UK achieving a stated target of having the best superfast coverage in Europe by 2015.

In an age of austerity, home-working has much to commend it – delivering benefits to workers, the economy, businesses, customers, and even the environment. CCA members are at the forefront of some exciting home-working pilots that have delivered very impressive results. The next chapter is already underway and undoubtedly will prove equally fascinating.

Caveat: it doesn't work all the time

It's worth looking, at this stage, at the possibility that people unconsciously pay lip service to flexible working when they aren't actually doing it. Andy Lake, consultant and author, confirms as much; he visits companies and talks to them about flexible working and they say they're doing it when in fact, once he's dug a little, he realizes they are not.

Some of this is because of the culture in which people operate. Even government policy in the UK contributes to this: since the mid-2000s the law has said that people with children under 6 are allowed to ask to work flexibly if the business lends itself to that pattern. Later this was expanded to encompass all workers.

Let's pull back a second. You were only allowed to ask – that's 'ask', not ask successfully – according to the law, if your circumstances made you an exception. That's actually corporate governance by exception and frankly it's not going to work – if flexibility is going to run through an organization and produce results then you don't need to start by dividing people into 'may work flexibly' and 'may not'.

Lake says the other issue is partial flexibility. 'It can come from technology or it can come from HR, and they're not integrated,' he says. He has seen clients as a result where 'you get a series of disjointed initiatives, so you might end up with an office where they've opted for mobility because they have the technology but they haven't looked at the processes so it's not really flexible working'. It's not driven from the top so it's not truly integrated, he says.

The fact that it's often exception-based is also not positive.

Issues with flexibility

Governance by exception is a problem – everyone needs to be able to work flexibly, not just people who work from a given criteria.

It has to come from the organization overall and not just from HR, or just from IT.

Processes are as important as the technology.

Action points
for professionals

Understand this isn't just another one of those irritating changes management puts into place from time to time – this is a means of putting you and your needs firmly at the centre of your place of work.

Understand what sort of person you are.

Take an active part in any workplace surveys – this is where you have a genuine say in what needs to change. If the business is any good they'll do it more than once but the first survey is likely to be the big one.

Take full advantage of any training that's put in place and feed back, feed back – they need to know what's working.

Like the managers, enjoy the process. This is the part of your career in which your job becomes more fun than ever.

Action points
for managers

Orchestrate or provoke a wholesale change throughout the organization. Remember it needs to cover bricks, bytes and behaviours although probably not in equal measure – behaviours is the one that needs to change the most for the rest to start delivering.

Ensure you provide leadership through communication, through trust and through a thorough understanding of what your organization is and needs to be.

Dismiss the idea of human resources – this is human realization, you're helping people reach their potential.

Survey, implement, survey, repeat. Regularly.

Establish new behaviours among the middle managers as well as the seniors.

Train the associates or staff.

Enjoy the process – this should make your business a better place to be.

Afterword

HR DOES NOT STAND FOR HUMAN RESOURCES ANY MORE...

The authors of this book would like to leave you with a thought. Names of departments change over the years. There used to be complaints, now it's the more comforting 'customer relations'. There used to be personnel, now it's human resources.

It sounds very impressive – until you start to break it down. You're no longer a person, you're a resource. Resources are things you use up and then when they're spent you get rid of them. This, to our minds, is not what people are about at all, it's what business can be about at its worst. And if we can set one thing right here then it's the balance between the people and the organization. The company, the social business, the local authority, whatever you work for, is important – we're not some sort of idealistic pair of hippies trying to stick it to The Man. We are, however, aware of the importance of the individual, the person who can develop in the midst of an organization. Who can find a better balance between their work and every other element of their life, who can function as only they can and be the best version of themselves they have ever been. This is not the world of 'human resource' to be chewed up and spat out like any other sort of resource.

This is a world in which HR stands for human realization.

This is the world in which a business makes its money by investing in its people and making sure they're enjoying what they do. It's a world in which people adopt specific techniques for building mutual trust between themselves and their colleagues. It's a world in which the workplace is wherever the task is best completed, not wherever the company happens to have paid a hefty rental. It's a world of smarter working, and it's something to strive for.

By all means we said 'strive'. If one lesson has emerged from this book then we hope it's that none of this is easy. It requires evaluation of the current bricks, bytes and behaviours, and actionable points after this has happened. It needs a careful focus on the four C workspaces – contemplation, communication, concentration and collaboration. There will be a need for acoustic zoning, for ensuring the right people are working dispersed and there will be the certainty that nothing is happening by accident or on an ad hoc basis – it all needs careful planning and staff buy-in as you go along.

It should also be fun. That's something we can't mention enough and we hope it's come out. Yes, it's hard work but getting the best out of people, making sure they enjoy their assignments and their colleagues as they move through their working lives should give a good manager one hell of a kick. The leader needs to be a business leader by all means but also a sort of master of ceremonies. You could compare it to a ringmaster in a circus; there will be times when everything looks just a bit chaotic and the onlooker might not be certain you're fully in control – but you know you are. You're aware of just where the acrobats and clowns are standing and you're confident they know their cues or rather, in this case, you know the mavens are in their right place, the evangelists are in the field and the relaters are explaining the new working culture internally to every stakeholder in the business – they may be on site, they may be elsewhere. You've trained them to communicate most effectively through every medium available to your organization so they can take account of a lack of body language or emotional content; they know what they're doing, you know how to keep the thing afloat, it's working and it will deliver.

Have fun – and let us know how you get on!

Bibliography

This book is intended as a new work, supported by case studies and expert interviews but the authors confirm they would have been nowhere without the considerable amount of work already available on our given subjects. The books and studies below are all referred to in the text and we have no hesitation in recommending them as further reading.*

Business Reimagined, Dave Coplin, Harriman House, 2013.

Charisma, Andrew Leigh, 2nd ed., Pearson 2012

The Digital Edge, McDonald and Rowsell-Jones, Gartner, 2012.

A Guide to Office Acoustics, British Association of Interior Specialists, 2011.

Home Working - Lost in Translation, Plantronics Research by Annie Leeson, 2011.

The Human Fabric, Bijoy Goswami, Aviri, 2004.

The Impact Code, Nigel Risner, Capstone 2006.

The Joy of Work, Warr and Clapperton, Psychology Press, 2009.

New Demographics, New Workspaces, Jeremy Myerson, Joanne Bichard, Alma Erilch, Gower 2012.

The Smart Working Handbook, Andy Lake, 2011.

Sound Business, Julian Treasure, Management Books, 2007.

Space to Work: New Office Design, Jeremy Myerson and Philip Ross, Laurence King 2006.

Speech Impact Course for Virtual Collaboration: Crawford Communications.

Speed Lead, Kevan Hall, Nicholas Brealey, 2008.

The Speed of Trust, Stephen M. R. Covey, Simon & Schuster, 2008.

This Is Social Commerce, Guy Clapperton, Capstone 2012.

Top Companies of the Future, CRF, 2008.

The Topology of Work: A Catalyst for Change, Plantronics Research, Annie Leeson, 2009.

What Color is Your Parachute?, Richard N Bolles, updated 2014, Ten Speed Press.

Work, Happiness and Unhappiness, Peter Warr, LEA, 2007.

* Author Guy is acutely aware he's accidentally ended up recommending his own books here...

About the authors

Guy Clapperton

Guy Clapperton has been a journalist first in the technology area and then in business journalism since 1989. He has contributed on these subjects to *The Guardian*, *The Times*, *The Financial Times*, *The Sunday Telegraph*, *The Independent* and numerous magazines. He has for some years written the fortnightly UC Insight bulletin for the Connected Business Show in London, formerly known as UC Expo.

In the book world Guy is the author of *Free Publicity for your Business in a Week* but more recently he wrote *This Is Social Media*, which stayed at the top of several Amazon best sellers lists consistently for three years from its publication in 2009. Its sequel, *This Is Social Commerce*, came out in 2012. In 2009 he also co-wrote *The Joy of Work?* with Prof. Peter Warr. He is part owner of Working Lives, a social network and employment hub for the blue collar community.

The social media books put him onto the speaker circuit and since 2010 he has presented on media and collaboration in 11 countries spanning two continents; in 2011 he became a member of the Professional Speaking Association, rising to Fellow in late 2012. If you want to contact Guy about speaking at an event he is available as Guy@Clapperton.co.uk.

Guy is also a broadcaster, having contributed regularly to programmes on BBC Radio London and the BBC World Service; he is currently to be seen commentating on the newspaper review section on the BBC News Channel on TV.

He has attempted a career in stand-up comedy but this is probably just a mid-life crisis thing, pay no attention.

Philip Vanhoutte

With a 35-year whirlwind career in the information and communications technology industry, Philip Vanhoutte lives and breathes flexible working.

Groomed at Accenture and Wang Labs as an energetic office automation consultant in the 80s and surfing the waves of the laptop revolution at Dell in the 90s, he has never used a professional desktop computer, forging the way for work via a laptop on the road and anywhere else his profession takes him.

In the early 2000s, as the Global Marketing Vice President at Sony-Ericsson, he launched the first smartphone with Bluetooth headset and reaps both the benefits and cruxes of a constant connection via mobile phone.

As the current Senior VP and Managing Director of Europe & Africa for Plantronics, his love for personal technology and wearables has matured into a passion for smarter working – one that he has manifested across the entire corporation. Over the past years he has researched and implemented radical new office changes globally to support the growing trend in agile working.

He now shares his learnings in The Smarter Working Manifesto and continues to evangelize the movement to give associates the freedom to work where and when works best and help employers identify the right working environment for their teams.

Philip Vanhoutte is the chairman of the Leesman Advisory Board and in 2013 he received a lifetime achievement award from the UK Contact Centre Association.

Notes

....

....

....

....

....

....

....

....

....

....

....

....

....

www.smarterworkingmanifesto.com

Notes

....

....

....

....

....

....

....

....

....

....

....

....

....

www.smarterworkingmanifesto.com

Notes

....

....

....

....

....

....

....

....

....

....

....

....

....

....

Notes

....

....

....

....

....

....

....

....

....

....

....

....

....

www.smarterworkingmanifesto.com

Index

SUNMAKERS

Publish your expertise

 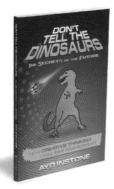 

 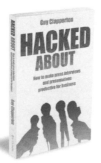 

www.sunmakers.co.uk